BRUNO SAMMARTINO
An Autobiography of Wrestling's Living Legend

Bruno Sammartino
with
Bob Michelucci and Paul McCollough

IMAGINE,INC./Pittsburgh

BRUNO SAMMARTINO
An Autobiography of Wrestling's Living Legend

by Bruno Sammartino
with
Bob Michelucci
and
Paul McCollough

An original publication of IMAGINE,INC.

IMAGINE,INC.
P.0. Box 9674
Pittsburgh, PA 15226

Front and back cover photographs by Jim Shafer

ISBN: 0-911137-14-9

Library of Congress Number: 89-81625

First IMAGINE,INC. Printing: June, 1990

Printed in the U.S.A.

DEDICATION

This book is dedicated with all of
my love to my mom

ACKNOWLEDGEMENTS

The author(s) and publisher gratefully acknowledge the following individuals and companies for their assistance.

Frank Amato, Don Antal, Margie Antal, Bill Apter, Eric Caiden, Bill Cardille, Debra Ciarelli, Civic Arena Corporation, Bob Conley, Frank Diaz, Lynne Dyer, Rita Eisenstein, Hollywood Book & Poster, Pat Jefferies, Joe Katrencik, Phil Levine, Diana Michelucci, Brad Morris, George Napalitano, National Wrestling Alliance, Tom Rooney, Carol Sammartino, Jim Shafer.

FOREWORD

When I was a very young kid, growing up in Italy, I used to hear stories about people who had been to America. They said that the streets were paved with gold and as a child, I took that literally. I really thought you could reach down and scoop up handsful of the stuff.

Of course, when I did come to the United States at age fourteen and saw that the streets weren't paved with gold, I began to understand what those who had come before me had meant. Their meaning in the saying was that here, in America, is the land of golden opportunity.

For me, a boy from another country, what did it mean coming to America? In reality, chances are that I would not have stayed in the town where I was born. Many like me left to go into the world because the war had devastated my village. Years later, as a professional wrestler, I met townspeople from my home in places like Australia, South America, all over. All of us had to leave that town to go and find work and to make a life for ourselves. We just couldn't do that anymore in Italy.

I feel that I was so lucky to come to this great country, America where I had the freedom to do what I wanted to do...learn to be a carpenter at the place where I got a job working construction...join the YMCA to train. I had the opportunity to come and practice with college wrestling teams so I could gain experience in what I love best and then become a professional wrestler. I feel lucky even just getting the chance to cut the grass.

As the old saying goes, 'Only in America' and in this great country. I believe that America gave me the opportunity to go on with my dream, which was to be a champion. I was able to give my family a much better life than I ever experienced as a youngster. Today, even though I'm retired, I still sometimes wake up and I'm afraid somebody's going to pinch me and tell me it was all a dream, and that I'm not in America but back in the mountains, starving, hiding from the German troops.

Even with all of the traveling that I've done, and I've visited countries with great beauty and tremendous histories, I can honestly say that I've never been anywhere in the world that could come within a mile of the United States of America. This is truly the greatest country in the world. I thank God and I thank my Dad every day of my life for giving me the chance to live in this land. For me it is a privilege to be an American.

MY EARLY YEARS IN ITALY

I was born in a little mountain town in Italy called Pizzoferrato on October 6, 1935. The youngest in my family, I was also the biggest, weighing more than eleven pounds at birth.

My Dad, Alfonso, was a blacksmith by trade. When I was only three months old, in January of '36, he left Italy for America. He returned there to work and earn enough money to buy land on which he could build a home for his wife and family.

Concerta was my Dad's older sister and she and her husband had immigrated to the Pittsburgh area. So Dad came to live with her in an area they called Little Italy. Now it's known as Panther Hollow.

My Dad was born in January, 1891 so he would have been 45 when he came over that time. He used to tell me that in those days it was easy to find work in America. Workers were needed everywhere. He said that eight or nine men from the same town might come over and board with Italian families who were already here. They might only have a mattress on the floor but they would eat well, have a place to stay and still be able to send money back home.

Dad told me that blacksmiths were used in construction then. He would use his skills to fix shovels, picks and other equipment that got broken. He did that for a time then later on he went to the steel mills. He worked very hard, trying to save every dime he could.

A couple times before 1936, my Dad had traveled to the United States. He would work for a while and then come back and be with his family. What happened that last time was that the War started and passages were closed. We were stuck in Italy and Dad was stuck in America. For long periods of time there could be no communications whatsoever. And if you knew my Dad, the kind of guy he was, I think that he went through every bit as much hell as we did, not knowing, hearing about fighting going on, learning about casualties.

So in Italy it was my mother, Emilia, who kept the family together while my dad was away. I lived there in our stone house with my older brother, Paul, and my older sister, Mary.

To show you how things were when I was young, there were no doctors in Pizzoferrato and many children and adults got sick and often died from probably nothing more than the flu virus. Simple medications could have saved lives back then, but none were available and so many perished at early ages.

2

I lost a sister, Annita, when she was thirteen and a brother, Sandrino, when he was only two. My mother had also borne twins, but sadly, they too passed away shortly after birth.

We had a field where we grew nearly all of our food. Just about everything we ate, wheat, corn, potatoes, we raised right there.

Because we were very high up in the mountains, we used to get an enormous amount of snow in the winter. We would be literally snowed in for months due to these severe snow storms. So we had to make provisions for this in the early fall.

The basement of our house was divided into sections and it was there we kept our potatoes, wheat, flour, corn or whatever. Then, when the snows did come, we were just stuck in the house. We had our food and fire and just waited for the storms to stop.

The doors to our house opened to the inside, not like they do here. The reason for this was that you would have to dig yourself a tunnel to get to the street because the wind would drift the snow higher than the door.

There was no work to be done in winter since everything was paralyzed by the snow so when we could get out, we went skiing.

As a child, this life was for me very normal. I played with the other children when I could and I worked when I had to, which was a great deal of the time in the Spring, Summer and Fall. I would go with my brother and sister to the fields where we would help our mother with the crops. That was my childhood until late 1943 and the beginning of 1944.

The War started out rather simply for us. When the first Germans came to our town, they came in small groups. They were regular German Army and were merely scouting the area for good military positions. They didn't bother us or show us any hostility so we thought little of it.

A few would appear occasionally to check out different areas in our mountains. You see, Pizzoferrato had only a population of 900 or so, but from its position you could see many other villages just like mine. We used to walk from one to the other or go by horse and buggy, but for the Germans the important thing was rapid mobility. They needed to know all about our roads and our resources.

Several weeks later, after the first contacts with the Germans, one night we were awakened by what sounded like the whole town coming apart. Unbelieveable roaring noises. Dozens, maybe hundreds of armored cars and jeeps rolled through our town.

We were completely dumbfounded. We had never even seen so much as an automobile before this happened, although before the war, I do recall seeing a small truck having a difficult time winding its way around the narrow and tricky roads. The Germans came like a storm, sweeping aside everything in their path.

Along with all their noise came a fierce pounding on our door. It was Uncle Camillo, married to my mother's sister, he was one of the kindest human beings I have ever known. He was just like a father to us kids, a gentle man. This night he had come to warn us that the SS, the storm-troopers themselves, had moved into our area.

We realized that the SS were quite unlike the first soldiers who had occupied our town. The SS wanted the town only for themselves, and they wanted the townspeople out. These troops became extremely violent when their wishes weren't met immediately and many of our people perished under their heel. We fled with just the clothes on our backs.

One of my Mom's brothers, also named Alfonso like my Dad, owned a little cabin out in the fields. One of my strong memories is heading toward that cabin, running like crazy and scared as anyone can be. Fortunately, we made it to Uncle Alfonso's without incident, but my Mother began to feel uncomfortable there.

You see, my Uncle Camillo had joined with the partisans. His group and others like them linked up with the Allies to help direct them through the mountainous terrain. And the war crept closer to us each day.

Pizzoferrato, Italy where I was born.

4

A birdseye view shows the rugged terrain of Pizzoferrato.

English soldiers, in another nearby town to us called Castell, were bombing the area with cannons. Because the English weren't sure of the German positions, at times we ended up in the line of fire. My mother said to us, "My God, if one of those bombs hits this little shack here, we'll all be killed!"

So she decided that we would head towards the big mountain called Valla Rocca. She had gotten word that many of our friends and relatives from Pizzoferrato who had escaped the SS were hiding there. They felt it was a safe place that the Germans wouldn't dare bother with because it was such a difficult and treacherous climb.

My Aunt, Alfonso's wife, wanted no part of Valla Rocca. She was determined that she and her children were going to stay in that little cabin and rely on God's will to survive. My Mother, on the other hand, was a person who believed that the Lord helps those who help themselves.

As the artillery fire continued to draw closer, we began to experience bombings from the air. Finally, my Mother grabbed me and my brother and sister and said, "Enough. We're heading toward the big mountain...Valla Rocca."

I've often been asked how I can remember this so vividly since I was so young when it occurred. All I can tell you is that nine years old is old enough to remember the feelings that you had when such fantastic things happen to you. You couldn't forget them if you tried.

As we were racing to the mountain, my Mother would try her best to keep us all together. Every so often bombs would hit close by and actually pick us up off the ground. We seemed to be running first in one direction, then in another.

I can remember an incident that I suppose now we can look back and talk about it and laugh, but it sure wasn't funny at the time. As I said, it did seem as if the bombs were exploding all around us, when in reality, they were probably much further away. In any case a huge chunk of dirt came flying through the air and hit my sister Mary square in the back, knocking her down. She began to scream hysterically that the bomb hit her. She thought that a piece of shrapnel had ripped into her. Of course, it had been just a hunk of dirt.

My Mother just grabbed her and hollered at me and Paul to stay together. Hold hands, she told us and just stay close together. So we kept running.

We knew we weren't going to make it to the top of the mountain in one day, so we stayed at the bottom all night, hiding. We had no food, no lights, nothing. My Mother, poor Mama, stayed awake, watching over us, worrying about the Germans, wolves and other animals that might harm us.

As soon as dawn broke, we started to make the climb. It seemed to take forever to reach the top of that mountain. We were all so very hungry and tired, but we kept going until finally we made it.

I remember seeing paths cut into the woods by those who had arrived before us. And they had constructed shelters that resembled Indian teepees, or maybe more accurately, like the long houses that you have seen in the history books. The men had taken small trees and made logs from them, using the logs to erect the shelters. At the top was a hole for the smoke of the fire to rise through and there would be just one entrance. It was almost a barracks with the cracks sealed with mud and stones.

One of our neighbors, who had already built some of these shelters for his own family, was aware that my Dad was far away in America. He realized that this poor woman, Emilia, and her three children were desperately in need of a place to stay, so he allowed us stay stay in one of these cabins.

The inside of these buildings were partitioned. Logs would be used as dividers to section off areas for separate families and believe me, there were many people crammed into that small area.

My Mother and Brother and Sister and I shared a tiny living space that barely allowed us room to lie down and sleep. I remember that the Fall had brought the chill air so a fire would be burning in the middle of the cabin to keep us all warm. We didn't have a lot of blankets to go around and we

6

were always cold. I would watch the smoke rise from the fire and escape through the hole in the roof. We were stuck there, just waiting.

As far as food and clothing went, everybody was on their own. Really there was no such thing as being neighborly. Most of the people there weren't concerned with helping one another. They were just trying to figure out ways for them and their families to survive.

At night, many times my mother would hike down Valla Rocca to make her way back to our house, which was now occupied with German troops who lived and slept there. She would sneak into our house through the back door, using the key which she still had in her possession. Then she would creep into the basement where we kept the food and fill her sack with our own provisions.

She took whatever she could as quickly as she could. Sometimes it was potatoes or corn. Other times it may have been flour. She would hurry back with this food for us kids to eat.

My mother at this time was no young woman either. She was forty-eight years old and making so many of these trips up and down that mountain. But our food situation was desperate. That's why she also went by herself, too. It was less dangerous than going with one or two others.

Of course, my mother wasn't the only adult who made these trips back into Pizzoferrato. Still, everybody was on their own who went on them.

When my mother would go down the mountain, she would always time it out so that she would get into town late at night when the Germans were sleeping. There were guards naturally, but she knew the town inside and out, so she could avoid them fairly easily. She risked her life for us like this about once a week.

One time she was captured and put onto a truck with other prisoners The back of that truck was rimmed with barbed wire, but that didn't stop my Mom. She actually dove through it and was shot at, but she ran like the devil and hid in the dense woods that she was so familiar with. The Germans couldn't find her and she returned to us alive and well.

And once, as she was leaving town a German soldier spotted her, and he shot her, hitting her in the shoulder. She ran and dodged and got away from the soldier. She was a woman possessed. She knew she had those three children, waiting for her on top of that mountain, and that their survival depended solely on her. Nothing would stop her from returning. Nothing.

I remember those times when Mom would leave us. We'd hear the bombs exploding down below. We weren't even sure where the shells were hitting, since there were many, many towns all over the area that were occupied and involved in the fighting.

7

We would be petrified when she left, just worrying about whether she would return or not. Her trips usually would take two or three days, sometimes longer. While she was away, me and Paul and Mary would sit on the edge of the mountain, where we could look down to see someone returning. And we just stared. No matter how hungry we were or how miserable the weather was, it all didn't matter when we would spot our Mom coming back up. I remember this as though it were yesterday. Oh, my God, what a feeling that was...to see her coming back!

From high atop the mountain, one could see the rooftops of the homes.

That's how we would survive. If my Mom had stolen some potatoes, she would put them on the fire, and each of us would eat one potato. Another time, we would have a single ear of corn. If she did get some flour, she would take water and make dough, and even though we had none of the other ingredients to go with it, there would be bread. Everything was rationed out so it would last.

There were times when we didn't get to eat at all, sometimes for days. Because there was so much fighting going on in the villages, my Mom would have to stay away. When there was no food, we would fill our bellies with snow. I remember stuffing myself with snow many times. When the weather started to warm up, we would eat the Spring dandelions and whatever other greens we could find. So many of the older people that were with us died off because there was nothing to eat but these things.

All the while we were hiding on Valla Rocca, the countryside still echoed from the bombings and we knew that many fierce battles were being fought. The Germans were being driven back and kept moving closer to us. In fact, the Germans did an exceptional job in holding on to our towns. It seemed

8

that every time the British would try to advance, they would be beaten back. The Germans had the positioning advantage because of the terrain.

The Germans had also dug holes in the roads that were nearly the size of a room, then covered them up so cleverly that, as the Allied soldiers would cross these excavations, they would plunge into them and then the Germans would just machine-gun them down. The number of people killed was unbelievable. Eventually, many of our people, especially the men, were able to help the British maneuver through our rough mountain roads.

The Germans, of course, were interested in finding out where we and others like us were hiding. They wanted to put a stop to any efforts to help the British.

Once three German soldiers did discover our sanctuary. They came on horseback as far as they could, then climbed up the rest of the way on foot. All the men, what few there still were with us, that day were out hunting for food. We were defenseless.

These SS men set up a machine gun and they lined up all of our people from the mountain against a rock wall. Beaten down by our hunger and sickness, we offered little resistance.

As I look back on that moment, I realize that my Mom was the bravest woman I've ever known. She was totally aware of what was happening. As kids, I'm not sure to this day if we fully understood what the Germans were about to do.

Mom had my brother and sister on one side of her and me, the youngest, on the other side, and she had her arms around all of us. She had no fear for herself. Her compassion was completely for us and she talked softly while the SS men were readying the machine gun to kill us.

She said, "Don't be afraid, my children...because soon we'll be in Heaven. And there will be no more cold, no more hunger, no more suffering. We'll all be together and we will be happy. It's going to be Paradise."

Luckily for us all, a couple of the hunters returned just in time. They saw what was happening and somehow managed to get behind the Germans without alerting them. On a silent signal, they rushed the three SS men and with knives, killed them, and saved our camp.

We were able to take possession of the machine gun and all of the ammunition that the Germans had brought up the mountain. This gun was to be our defense, in case more like them would find us. As it turned out, others did spot us. But they would be on horseback, see that the climb was too steep and turn around and go back down, just forgetting about those people who lived so high in the clouds.

Sometime, during all these hardships, I caught pneumonia. I guess starvation and the war had taken its toll on me. It was clear that I was dying.

My mother was so worried about me. She had already lost four children and did not want to lost a fifth. When my brother and sister had died, there had been a doctor who would visit once a month from Villa Santa Maria. That was all the medical help that was available in our village then but now, of course, on top of Valla Rocca, there were no doctors at all...not even once a month.

Some people laugh at those remedies that the old-timers talk about, but tall tale or not, my mother took steps to save my life using those long ago methods. She wrapped me up in whatever blankets she could find. Then she boiled water in a borrowed pot and placed dampened blankets around me which created a steambath effect. After a good steaming, she uncovered me and placed leeches all over my back. The theory was that these leeches would suck all of the poisoned blood from my system.

You may call this a lot of bologna, but all I know is that as sick as I was, I should have died...but I didn't.

We lived on the mountain top for nearly fourteen months. When we got word that the Germans had finally moved out of our town, we were elated. They left, not because they had been whipped, but because they had been completely cut off from their supplies so they had to retreat to the north.

Many people in our camp had died during this time...from sickness and starvation. I remember the hell that it was for my own family. My brother Paul and sister Mary were certainly not in the best of health after all we had gone through.

Because I was still too weak to walk on my own, my Mom had to carry me all the way down the mountain. We were all suffering from the effects of our long exile, but she got us back home with the same determination she had shown in keeping us alive all those months.

When we reached Pizzoferrato, we were devastated to see the destruction from the bombings. Everything lay in ruins and there were bodies everywhere.

You know, I remember seeing so many corpses of our own people, of the Germans, English and some Polish and all those dead bodies didn't really make an impression on me then. I know it sounds hard to believe but it's the God's truth. We had lived through so much hell that nothing else seemed to make an impact.

So the townspeople who had survived and returned began to clean up the village, starting first with the removal of all the dead to a burying site. Later, I began to think about the soldiers who had died in my town. Nobody knew who they were. They became just faceless people buried in unmarked graves all over the hillsides. What of their families?

We found out quickly that we could return to our own house and live in it, even though parts of it had been blown apart. Even though the fighting had moved away, problems brought on by the war continued. Practically everything had to be rebuilt and the Germans had ransacked our village, taking everything they could when they left.

There were still no doctors and many kinds of sicknesses erupted, most likely the result of the decaying bodies harboring germs. Ammunition had been left all over the streets and people were being killed from accidentally stepping on hidden landmines...and children were getting maimed and worse from picking up live grenades.

It took time but the townspeople cleaned up Pizzoferrato and began to rebuild from the ground up. We started to plant new crops, too. And I slowly regained my health, thanks to being back in our home and with my mother taking such good care of me in every way she could, scraping up a little bit of food here and there for us to eat, watching over me with her love. It took months but I got better, thanks to her.

COMING TO AMERICA

It was quite some time before we were able to communicate with my Dad again. As I had said before, I was born in October of 1935, and within three months of my birth, he had gone to America. I never knew what my Dad looked like because I had never seen a picture of him. In my part of the world, we didn't have cameras.

It wasn't until the war was over that my Mom finally got word through to him. He found out that we were all well and alive and in his return messages to us, he described what hell he had gone through, not knowing the fate of his family. He said he had tried to get news through the Italian newspapers and radio programs, but that all he would hear about was the bombings and how the Germans had overrun our town. As we suffered in hiding, his private hell came from not knowing where we were or even if we were still alive.

My Mom tells me that she discussed with my Dad about whether or not he should return to Italy and care for us. She told him flatly that the only thing left in the Old Country was misery, and if there were any way for us to come to America, we would all be better off.

I remember hearing the stories of streets paved with gold in America and that it was a country full of mansions and of people who were filthy rich. So when my mother told us that we were going to go to the United States to be with our father, we were all elated.

It wasn't until 1948 that our chance to leave materialized. Now at that time, all passage had to be arranged according to a quota system. I'm not sure to this day what that really meant or how it worked, but unfortunately, I didn't pass the physical and so we had to wait until our number came up again.

Of course, we were disappointed. While we waited, my health improved to the point where I was given a clean bill of health when our chance came around again...in 1950. We were on our way to America at last.

First we had to travel to Naples where we would catch our ship. Although I was fourteen years old then, it was the first time that I had ever left Pizzoferrato with its population of nine hundred. When we arrived in Naples, I was stunned by the size of this magnificent and awesome city.

The first thing we did was hurry to look at the ship that would carry us across the Atlantic. Our ship was one of two liners that were docked in Naples. They were nicknamed the twin ships, the Saturnia and the Locania and supposedly they had served in battle in the Middle East.

When we first saw our ship, the Saturnia, at first I didn't even realize that it was a ship. It looked so big to me I thought I was looking at another city. My mother assured me that it indeed was what was going to take us to our Dad in America.

Finally, after several days of waiting, on February 15, 1950, we boarded and steamed out of Naples. The trip was incredible. I couldn't decide which was worse, this voyage or the war. It took us fourteen days to reach New York and they were fourteen horrible days, let me tell you.

I admit I don't know much about ships but I sure know that the Saturnia was no luxury liner. We lived for those two weeks at the very bottom of the darn thing. Down there it was one big open floor that was divided by curtains. We all slept in bunks and there was this large piece of canvas which you would circle around your bed. My brother was on the bottom bunk and I was on the top, while my sister had the bottom of the other bunk with my Mom sleeping above her. Although not quite as bad, the arrangement reminded me of the small space we had shared during the war up on the mountain. I guess that this was the most economical way that my Dad could afford to bring us to the States.

When we went up on deck, we would climb up flights of stairs to get there. Looking back now, I'm sure there were different levels of accomodations where people with more money were traveling a little better than we were. But being young, I didn't know that and so accepted our quarters as just being the way you traveled on the high seas.

On our first day or two out, we were able to move about the ship whenever we wanted. Then the sea became so choppy that everyone in our section was confined down below. Ironically, even though I was the sickly one, my brother Paul was hit the worst with sea sickness, although

Paul, Mary and Bruno

13

my sister Mary came in a close second.

Because my mother and I weren't quite as affected, we had to play nurse-maids to them. They couldn't even go to the bathroom they were so knocked out. And of course they couldn't walk up the flights of stairs where the meals were served.

Mom and I would walk up those narrow stairs to the floor where the food was and we would find somewhere to sit down and eat. The tables had little boards all around the edges to keep the food and dishes from falling off as the ship pitched and rolled. We would then take something back down to my brother and sister so they could have some nourishment.

It had to be the worst time of the year to be making an ocean voyage. We were locked in most of the time because the seas were so rough. I remember that when we approached land coming through the Mediterranean and out past Gibraltar, the seas calmed somewhat and then some member of the crew yelled down to us to come above quickly and get some fresh air.

My brother and sister were still stretched out in their bunks, not moving, along with many others down there with us. Even though my Mom and I weren't all that much better off, we made our way up on deck. Up there, we sat down on crates and Mom kept repeating to me, "Take deep breaths, Bruno. The ocean air is fresh and good for the lungs."

This terrific sea air actually began to make me sick and I started to feel nauseated. In a short time, the seas got rough again and we were sent back down to our area.

It seemed as though we spent the rest of the trip there, resting, thinking about our new life, rolling and tossing in the high seas. What kept me going, of course, was the excitement about meeting my dad.

When we finally drew near the States, the seas calmed once more and again we were permitted up top. Even my brother and sister started to feel better as we neared New York harbor.

A big disappointment to us was that we missed seeing the Statue of Liberty. We arrived at night, and for some reason we were confined to our quarters and not allowed above until the next morning, long after we had passed Miss Liberty.

The next day, mass confusion reigned. All of our fellow passengers had come back to life and everyone was rushing to get off the ship and meet their loved ones. It had been a long and difficult journey for us and we were all glad it was over.

Once disembarked, we all headed to a nearby section of the docks where huge letters of the alphabet were posted. We were directed to go and stand under the letter that corresponded with the first letter of our last name. So we went, dragging our bags and whatever else we had with us and waited under the big 'S' for Sammartino.

We stood under the 'S' for what seemed an eternity. My mother, sister and brother all looked one way and I faced the other. Even though I had no idea what my father looked like, in my mind I pictured him as a tall, husky guy. I did know that he was no longer a young man, being close to fifty-nine years old in 1950.

Then I saw what looked to me to be a very old man shuffling toward us. He wore a tattered hat and eyeglasses. I never even looked at my mother to ask if this man was our father. Nothing. I just stood there staring as he walked closer and closer to us.

While the others were peering off into the opposite direction, this old man came up to us and softly called out my mother's name, "Emilia?"

She whirled around and screamed, "Alfonso! Alfonso!" and that's how I realized that here was my Dad, in the flesh.

He seemed overjoyed to see us. Still, he seemed more like a stranger than my father. I couldn't believe it. I knew it was going to take quite a bit of adjustment to get used to him.

One of our first family portraits taken in America.

Later that day, we took a train to Philadelphia. My Dad's sister and her

15

husband and family lived there so we stopped briefly before heading to Pittsburgh. Of course it was my first train ride. As we pulled into the Philadelphia train station, we heard the sirens of fire engines racing close by. It sounded almost like the war, the sirens blowing madly to tell us the bombs were coming. It shook me up pretty good but my Dad explained to me that in America, when a fire starts, these special trucks rush to it and put out the flames with water. The explanation sounded good, but the noise of the sirens still scared me.

Alfonso and Emilia Sammartino reunited in the United States.

We stayed there just one day, visiting and sight-seeing. My Aunt and Uncle drove us all around, showing off Philadelphia, a city they were proud of. I looked everywhere for the streets of gold and the castles and was disappointed when I didn't see any. I quickly learned that what you hear as a kid isn't necessarily the whole truth.

The next day we boarded another train bound for Pittsburgh. By now I was an old hand at train rides and as I watched the countryside whisk by,

I couldn't wait for the miles to pass, anxious to reach our new home. Maybe Pittsburgh was the place for mansions and golden highways.

As it turned out, my Dad had purchased an old house in the Oakland section of town on Cato Street, perched on a hill, right above the smokestacks of the steel mills. He had agreed to pay $6000 for the property, taking out a long term mortgage.

In those days, Pittsburgh's reputation as a dirty, smokey city was no exaggeration and we lived right in it. Believe me, I was disillusioned...not that I regretted coming to America, but it sure wasn't what I had envisioned.

Our home back in Italy may have been damaged by the war, but even so, it was well constructed out of heavy stone. Of course, it didn't have inside toilets or running water or many of the luxuries of an American home, but at least where we lived there was clean air and sunshine.

When we walked into our new home on Cato Street, what I saw was plaster falling down, wallpaper peeling away and instead of mountain stones, we had brick and wood. I wondered for a while what we had gotten ourselves into.

Our new home on Cato Street in Pittsburgh.

We were one of the first Italian families to move into this section of Pittsburgh. Formerly the area was predominately inhabited by Polish, Irish and Jews. When we arrived, the Jewish people were just starting to move out and relocate in Squirrel Hill. Most of the other Italians were living in a place called Panther Hollow or 'Little Italy.'

For the first few days, many of my Dad's friends and relatives started stopping over to meet us and it was wonderful to see them all. Then, after things settled down, my Brother, Sister and I were enrolled in school because my Dad wanted us to learn English right away. We attended Schenley High

17

School which was about a two and a half mile walk from our house.

As we started our schooling, for the first time in my life I experienced prejudice. As we walked to our classes, we would be continually taunted and called names like 'dago' and 'wop'. We would even be beaten up because of our heritage.

In the old country, this kind of behavior didn't exist. We were all Italians. If you argued with one another, there were no ethnic slurs tossed at you.

It was different here in America. We didn't understand what these names meant, but we knew they weren't respectful. The whole experience taught us much.

We were so grateful for having come to the great America but at the same time we were getting our noses bloodied for just being ourselves. My God, we had gone through a war and worried every minute about getting killed, and now in the land where the streets were supposed to be paved with gold, we got beaten up for our accents. But we would survive. We always did.

Let me just say a word here about my brother, Paul. We've always been extremely close. We knew how near we both came to death from the war and that's what drew us into such a tight bond. We never really fought much the way young boys are known to fight. We just seemed to like each other an awful lot.

Paul and I at Christmas.

My brother and I have always been very close.

As we grew up, Paul became the responsible one. He always seemed to be older and wiser than his years. I remember that if my Mother would want us to go to the fields and bring some vegetables in for the supper table, Paul would be the one in charge even though he was only seven or eight. My Mom could always trust him to do the things that I wasn't quite old enough or mature enough to do.

When we had these hard times in the beginning of our new life in Pittsburgh, Paul always played the big brother. I certainly got beaten up more than he did. Since he was a little huskier, he would stand up for me. This he did even though he was nearly as undernourished from the war as I was when we first came over.

So our life began to settle into its routine and we learned our English. To my Dad this was the key for us...to be able to speak the language of the land.

Very quickly summer rolled around. My Mother, as usual, always had her boys' interests in mind. She had talked with a fellow by the name of Angelo Pasquerelli, who was a landscape contractor. Using her powers of persuasion, she was able to line me up with a job for the summer months, while my brother Paul worked for another contractor named Max.

Since my brother and I were both pretty frail boys, we wanted to do something about it. One Jewish kid named Maurice Simon, whom we had met at school, saw the shabby treatment we were getting from the others and felt sorry for us. He wanted to help so he suggested that we join the YMHA...the Young Men's Hebrew Association. If we did that, then he promised to show us how to exercise with weights and train to become stronger and healthier.

Using weights was something that we had never heard of before...and unfortunately, it cost money to join the Y. It was money we just didn't have.

When we both started working, on paydays we would turn our paychecks over to Mom and Pop because they were really struggling. Truly, my Dad was not in very good financial shape. The mortgage payment on the house was a significant monthly burden. His own mother was still alive and Dad was trying to support her, too. And he had his own brothers and sisters who needed help. So to help out, my brother and I would rarely keep any money for ourselves.

Until we could find the money to join the YMHA, Paul and I did scrape together enough money to send for the Charles Atlas strength-building course we read about in all the magazines. I think it cost five dollars.

I'll never forget those days. When we weren't working at our jobs, we would spend our days helping Dad knock the old peeling plaster down, then replaster the walls. We didn't have the money to hire a professional to do it for us.

Then in the evenings, Paul and I would sneak down into the basement and put our Charles Atlas course to use. We were learning all about 'dynamic tension' and doing push-ups by the hour. We were hiding from our parents because we were sure they would think us silly.

Finally, I approached my mother about joining the Y. The Charles Atlas course was fine as far as it went, but I wanted to get more serious about body building. I explained to her that here was a club in town which Paul and I could join that would make us husky, strong and healthy. Mom, without knowing anything more about it, thought that it was a good idea...since it had to do with exercise.

I told her that the membership fee was something like eleven dollars for each of us. She said perhaps we could keep a little bit of money from our paychecks for the cause. And that's exactly what we did. We saved until we had enough and then we joined.

You know, I always did feel more comfortable talking to my Mother than to my Dad. He certainly wasn't an unreasonable man, but he still seemed more like a stranger than a father to me.

My brother and I sit around the dinner table with Mom and Pop.

And so my brother and I began to train. It was a revelation to me. I became addicted to it. There was no other feeling in the world to compare with working out. I felt in my gut that this was something for which I was destined and that someday, somehow, it would do something in return for me.

At this same time, I began to develop an intense interest in wrestling, too. I guess my passions for both working out and wrestling grew out of my desire to never let myself get to be like the malnourished, skinny kid I was back during the war. It soon grew evident that I had wrestling in my blood. I swear to you that I must have been born with it.

At Schenley High, I would always try to get other guys to work out with me on the mat. Now at that time, in the early 1950's, there were no wrestling programs in the city schools, so the guys that I would wrestle with would be people I could pull in from my gym classes or from the football team after practice.

Schenley High School in Pittsburgh's Oakland Section.

Mister Gross was my gym teacher and also the football coach. He knew Rex Perry, who was the wrestling coach at the University of Pittsburgh then. He told Perry about this kid from the old country who simply loved to wrestle. Gross asked Perry if it would be all right to send him to workout with the college wrestling team...and believe it or not, Perry gave his okay.

I started as soon as I could. After school, I would walk from Schenley High to the Pitt Field House way up on top of what the local residents call "Cardiac Hill." The first few times I went, I ended up really feeling like an inferior being. I hadn't realized that Pitt had one of the finest wrestling teams in the country then. They had Hugh Perry, Rex's son, who went to the Olympic Games. Another son, Ed Perry, had won the National AU. A guy named Solomon had won in his class in the National AU. DeWitt was a fellow on the team who not only had won in the National AU but was a Pan American Games champion. I mean, these guys were great.

All of a sudden, from working out in a gym and beating up those highschool boys, I went directly to wrestling these nationally ranked college men. I'm thinking, boy, maybe I'm not so tough. Talk about getting an inferiority complex!

No one particular Pitt wrestler took me under his wing. It just didn't work out that way. Now I don't mean this in a negative sense. You have to realize

21

that these guys had academic responsibilities, too, in addition to training for meets. Many of them were on wrestling scholarships and they had to keep up with their grades as well as staying on top of their wrestling. I remember that some of them would stumble into practice with bloodshot eyes because they had to stay up the whole night before studying for a test. So with all that going on, there was just no time to take a special interest in some kid from high school.

Yet that didn't discourage me. It only made me more determined to work that much harder. When I first started, I thought Coach Perry was just going to say to me, "Get the heck out of there!" but he didn't. We went all through the wrestling season with me working out with the team. And when I couldn't practice at Pitt, for example if the team were off on an out-of-town trip, then I'd be at the Y, pumping iron.

I didn't live my life like a lot of guys my age. I remember some of my buddies teasing me about all the time I spent in training. While I was wrestling or pumping iron, my friends would be doing normal things like going swimming or taking a girl to the movies. It wasn't that I didn't have the desire to date, but first of all I was a very bashful kid. And too I had such a tremendous drive for what I was doing in the gym that I wasn't going to skip a session for anything. Every hour that I spent in training made me more determined that here was where my future lay. I admit, I became a person possessed.

As I progressed in my training, people started to look at me and take notice. I was growing larger and stronger. When I first arrived in America, I weighed slightly under 90 pounds. When I graduated from Schenley in 1955, I weighed 225 pounds. So you can imagine how well my hard work was paying off.

At one point, I was offered a scholarship myself to come and wrestle for Pitt. The deal was to be a year to year agreement and I only had to do two things annually for the scholarship to carry into the next year. I had to prove myself worthy as a wrestler and worthy as a student. If I didn't do well with either, then I was out.

But the arrangement never panned out. I never went on to college. My Dad had been talking to Carmen Tropea, an Italian contractor in the building trades in the Pittsburgh area. Some years back, Dad had worked for Carmen as a laborer.

He had asked Carmen if he could get his son, Bruno, into the union as a carpenter. My brother Paul had already gone out on his own and was now working as a cabinet maker, learning that trade.

Neither of us could afford college at the time. So since my Dad felt that joining the union was best for me, I followed his wishes. My brother Paul would later on join the service and after his hitch was up, go to college in the evenings under the GI Bill.

For me, there was another reason. I really didn't have much confidence in myself in academics. I'm sure it stemmed back to when we came over from the Old Country. We couldn't speak a word of English then and it took a lot of time and effort to master the language. Often when I would read books, there were many words that I couldn't understand the meaning of. It was a big handicap all through school.

My brother Paul though was an extremely bright student. While I was struggling to graduate with a C average, my brother sailed through with an A average all the way. He was always walking to the library to do research and to study.

Sometimes my Dad would say "Look at this, Bruno. Paul gets all A's. Why can't you get A's, too?" It was no use to tell my Dad that I just couldn't.

Don't get me wrong. I was never jealous of my brother. I really admired his accomplishments. I used to brag about how bright he was and about his scholastic honors.

So there it was. My Dad had lined up a job for me after graduation. What was I to do? I didn't want to disappoint my parents since opportunities for jobs like these were hard to come by. And I wasn't all that sure that I could make the grade in college...so I turned down the wrestling scholarship and accepted my fate. After graduation, I would learn the trade of carpentry.

Of course, I kept training. There was nothing that was going to stand in the way of that. When there was no wrestling at Pitt, we would shift our efforts over to the Y, where we had a wrestling ring set up. I used to coerce the guys who were wrestling at Pitt to come over and work out with me there.

Then I started to compete with the weights and I started winning contests. I began with the Novice, then advanced to the Junior, then to the Senior Stake meets, winning all those. I even went into a National Meet with my power lifting.

My brother Paul got to be pretty good with the weights, too. He topped the scales at about 215 and competed with me in many of the same meets. It was great to have him along at these competitions, encouraging me to push even harder.

So even though I wasn't going on to college, my dream stayed alive. I was going to make something of myself with my strength and dedication to training.

EARNING A LIVING

Thanks to my father's initiative, I started working soon after graduating from Schenley High School in June of '55 as a union apprentice carpenter for Mister Carmen Tropea. From the beginning I really didn't learn that much about carpentry. Since I was such a strong lad, the union crews were using me to load and unload trucks, to dig, pick, lift and carry. I did anything and everything but carpentry work.

Actually, I never complained. I was getting paid okay and I felt good about that. And no matter how many hours I worked during the day, even if I worked overtime, I'd rush home to Cato Street, grab something to eat, then hurry off to the Y...which was that two and a half mile walk.

I know kids today laugh at you when you tell them that you had to walk to school so many miles, but it was true. From my house to Schenley High School was two and a half miles, then the Y was right down the street from that. And I would walk back and forth, in rain, sleet, snow or sunshine...regardless of how hard I had worked that day at the building site. I vowed never to miss a workout under any circumstances.

In early July, my Mom came to me with some surprise news. She said that she had been actually saving money from the paychecks that my brother Paul and I had been handing over to her for the past few years. Now, she thought, there might be enough money to buy a car for me.

Mom was incredible. Here she was, putting away a dollar here and a dollar there until there was a nice-sized nest egg. And as luck would have it, our tenant, an auto mechanic by the name of Jimmy, who rented a room on the second floor in my parents' house, knew of a car for sale at the garage where he worked.

I went with him to look at it and it seemed fine...a '52 Chevy which I bought for $715. Little did I know how important that car was going to turn out to be.

I had a training partner by the name of Alex Philin. He was a tremendous weightlifter and really should have gone to the Olympics, but he got pushed around a little bit by politics. In the Olympic games, if two competitors tie in the amount of weight lifted, then the rules say the person who is of lighter body weight gets selected. Alex had done exactly that...had tied another American lifter and was in line for Olympic selection because he was the lighter of the two...but the other athlete was picked. You figure it out.

At any rate, in the summer of '55, Alex was going steady with a girl named Lola who went to Oliver High School across town. He didn't have a car, which made visiting his sweetheart difficult. When he discovered that his good buddy Bruno had just bought a '52 Chevy, he seemed very happy for me. Why? Well, now I had the chance to bring these two lovebirds together.

So one early evening after we had just worked out, and shortly after I had purchased my car, Alex asked me if I could drive him over to see his girlfriend. I said sure and off we went. I dropped Alex off at Lola's and headed back to Cato Street.

A few days later, Alex asked me again if I could give him a ride to Lola's. I was beginning to wonder if I had started Bruno's taxi service.

We cruised over to Lola's and this time Lola had one of her girlfriends visiting her. I asked Alex, "Who is that girl with Lola?"

Alex leaned over and told me that the girlfriend's name was Carol. As soon as I had glimpsed her, standing there on the porch, something wonderful had happened. I just knew that I had to get to know Carol better. When I drove home that evening, my heart was pounding.

The first chance I had, I asked Alex if he could arrange for me to meet Carol. He teased me a little but agreed to do it. So the next time I ferried Alex over to Lola's, I parked the car and went inside with him.

I was introduced to Carol. She seemed even more beautiful than when I had first caught sight of her. It turned out that she was just 16 and was still attending High School.

Before I left later on that evening, I asked Carol if she would like to go to a movie with me and my friend, Alex, and her friend Lola. As it was in those days, Carol had to ask her parents for permission.

In short order, arrangements were made for me to meet her parents. They looked me over top to bottom and gave their approval. Yes, I could go out with their daughter.

After that, Carol and I and Alex and Lola were like the Four Musketeers, double-dating like crazy. Of course, Alex was completely in favor of the arrangement since he still didn't have a car and needed transportation.

As I had grown up in the Old Country, I had my own ideas about what sort of woman I would want to marry some day. Immediately, I felt that Carol was that person. I just liked the way she behaved, the way she did things...everything about her.

After a lot of double dates, I successfully ditched Alex and Lola one evening so I could take Carol out and talk to her alone. A little time had gone by since we had first met because she had just turned 17. When the opportunity came to tell her how I felt, I took full advantage of it.

In Old County style, I confessed to her that I hadn't been going out with very many girls because I had such a ridiculous training schedule...every

25

day wrestling, weightlifting and on top of that working a full-time job. I told her that I really liked her and that I would like to go steady with her.

Now for me going steady meant more than just seeing someone exclusively for a few months then moving on to another girlfriend. What it meant to me was that I wouldn't be seeing anyone else nor would she date other guys. The intent would be that when we could, we would get married. Carol liked the idea and so we started to go steady.

Throughout that Summer of '55, I continued working for Mister Tropea, saw Carol when I could and worked hard at my training. I started to gain some recognition from weightlifting...even setting some records. My local reputation got a boost when I began to appear on a local sports show in Pittsburgh, hosted by the great Bob Prince, the man who was to become nationally known as the "Voice of the Pittsburgh Pirates" after Rosey Rosewell retired.

These sports shows went out over KDKA TV. Bob had me demonstrate weightlifting on live television. Since I had competed in both Olympic and power lifting, I was able to show the audience a range of lifting styles. If you had watched me from show to show, you would have seen me getting a little tougher each time I appeared.

Then Summer turned to Winter and in December of '55, Mister Tropea had to lay off me along with a lot of other guys. There just wasn't enough work to go around. So when I wasn't helping out at home, I spent more and more hours in the gym and waited for Carmen to bring us back.

We didn't get called for months...not until early Spring of 1956 when Mister Tropea needed us to work on a Greek Church located right on the Boulevard of the Allies. The site was actually just a short distance from our house on Cato Street.

For as long as it lasted, it was good steady income. Then the axe fell again and by mid-Summer, I was laid off once more.

It was right around the time that my close friend and training partner decided we would go to 'the weightlifters picnic' regardless of the fact that we were both broke. Let me tell you what happened.

My best buddy was Freddy DeLuca and he was just a great weightlifter who competed in the 148 pound class. Like me, he usually worked a tough day, then trained all night. In his class he set all kinds of city and state records.

That particular time, late summer of '56, Freddy and I were both out of work and really pinching pennies. Despite that, we both wanted to go to York, Pennsylvania, for 'the weightlifters picnic.'

York was where Bob Opfman, the coach of all the Olympic weightlifters, owned the York Barbell Club. Each summer he would invite weightlifters

26

from around the country to come and compete at his Club. It was a lot of fun and it gave everyone a chance to see athletes from all over the nation go head to head.

Freddy and I had gone to York a couple of previous summers , but now we were ready for anything. We felt that both of us had gotten a lot stronger and we wanted to take on all comers. Unfortunately, we had a distinct cash flow problem.

At first, we had even set up an arrangement where four other guys would come with us to share the expenses, but at the last minute, everybody backed down. It was just Freddy and me and Freddy's gas hog of an Oldsmobile.

Posing on our front steps at Cato Street with a couple of buddies.

So we schemed about how we were going to pull this caper off. We budgeted everything down to the last cent. We figured how much gas it would take to get there and back. We made sure we had enough money to eat a meal or two and we allowed ourselves four dollars to find the cheapest motel room possible.

Off we went, driving straight through to York in one long day, pulling into town the night before the competition, searching for the cheapest room. After swinging past quite a few motels, we found one that charged only $2.50 for the night...but that was just for one person. We couldn't afford the room for two. Naturally Freddy checked in as a single while I hung around outside, making myself inconspicuous.

When we finally made it to the room, we both couldn't believe it. Even for $2.50 it was robbery. The room was smaller than most phonebooths. The sheets looked like they hadn't been changed since last summer. The top half of one window was busted out.

I told Freddy despite everything, I needed to get some sleep for the competition in the morning. I grabbed the blanket and slept on the floor and Freddy tried to fall asleep, lying on the broken mattress.

As we both lay there, trying to doze off, we kep hearing a very irritating noise that sounded like somebody chewing. Finally, Freddy couldn't take in anymore and switched the lamp back on. He looked down at the floor where he had put his shoes and there we saw we had a visitor. It was a huge rat, knawing at Freddy's leather shoes.

I jumped up and the rat scurried off to his hole. I gathered up my clothes and said to Freddy that there was no way I was going to spend the night in that room. Freddy scrambled for his belongings and we climbed back in the car, having spent probably less that two hours in our room.

We headed for York Park where everything was happening next morning and we slept in the grass that night. And we sure didn't get the greatest snooze let me tell you.

When we woke up the next morning, people were already pouring into the Park. We were both hungry so we went scouting for the cheapest food that the Park sold. That turned out to be hot dogs. We downed a couple of them apiece and headed for the competition.

Guess what? We both did great! I remember doing a bench press of 475 pounds which back then was an extraordinary lift. Freddy did very well for himself, too.

When the day was over and we were headed back to Pittsburgh in Freddy's Olds, we didn't even have enough money left for a victory

Here I am holding one of my many awards.

28

hot dog. But I was so elated over my performance that I really didn't feel the hunger or the tiredness. I had had such a good showing and had impressed so many of my fellow athletes that I felt like a celebrity...at least for the day.

On the way home, Freddy felt like he couldn't drive anymore so we switched. Soon after I started driving, I fell asleep at the wheel. The next thing I knew, I'd crossed over into the opposite lane of traffic. Freddy woke up just in time and started screaming and that woke me up real fast. My head jerked up and I saw cars coming straight at us. Freddy and I lurched for the wheel and we swerved back into our own lane. Believe me, that kept us awake for the rest of the trip.

In early Fall, just when it looked like I was going to be cooling my heels all winter with no work, I got a chance to hire on with the Henry Busey construction company. I had hoped that Carmen Tropea would get busy again but that hadn't happened. So I signed on with Busey, helping to build another church. I got a few months out of it and was laid off once more in November of '56.

My life as an apprentice carpenter was certainly having its ups and downs. I spent Christmas and New Year's unemployed, then in early February, I got a call to go work for the Johns Mansville company. That lasted nearly three months until early May of '57...and I was laid off yet another time.

By now my friend Freddy DeLuca has gone and joined the Air National Guard. From the moment he went in, he kept bugging me, saying, "Bruno, you ought to join the Guard. It's great, man."

"What's so great about it?" I asked him.

Freddy explained it to me. "Bruno, you know that the draft is going to get you if you just sit back and let it. Sooner or later you're going to get drafted into the service. That means two full years with no time off. You do that, you're going to miss the weightlifting training. You're going to miss the wrestling you're so crazy about. And what about the apprenticeship you're serving. You can kiss that all good-bye if you get drafted."

I shook my head. "So how can I not get drafted? It's inevitable. Like you say...sooner or later."

"Bruno, the Guard's the answer. You go away for basic training for four months, but then you get to come back home. After basic, you just go away two days a month till your hitch is up. What do you say?" Freddy grinned at me.

How could I knock down his logic? It all made sense. I drove out to the 112th Division, talked to the recruiting officer that and signed up. For basic training, I was assigned to Lackland Air Force Base, which is about twelve miles outside of San Antonio, Texas.

Now the Guard gives you a choice of what to specialize in, so since Freddy was in the Medics, I said, "That sounds great. Put me in the Medics." And I had a fine time in the Medics...learning how to take blood pressures, how to draw blood, how to tell what blood type you have, how to give shots.

Then one day, a certain Colonel comes around and he sees me conducting business very properly as a medic and says, "What the hell is this man doing as a medic?"

What he was reacting to was my build. I was 265 pounds, big and muscular, breaking records as a power lifter and the Colonel throws a fit because this strongman is being wasted as a medic. He immediately goes to the Sergeant in charge of the Air Police and demands that I be placed there. Quicker than you could say it, I was out of the Medics and into the Air Police.

Freddy was right. Going into the Guard was a very good move.

Here I am in basic training at Lackland AFB in Texas.

About six weeks after I came back from basic training in Texas, in early November of '57, I got very lucky and landed a job with Turner construction. Their big project was the building of the Hilton Hotel in downtown Pittsburgh. A union agent had me placed there. The Hilton was really the best site going at the time.

Once I got settled in and got to know the men on the crews, I felt right at home. The guys used to kid me about how strong I was and how much food I ate. It's certainly true that I had an enormous appetite. I used to go to work with a shopping bag filled with just my lunch. My Mom will tell you that she used to fix fourteen or fifteen sandwiches on homemade bread which she would cram into that shopping bag.

I probably drank seven quarts of milk a day. And when I came home at night my Mom would make loads of pasta for us. I'd almost never eat meat because we couldn't afford it. On rare occasions, we might eat chicken and then I could put away two whole chickens by myself. I guess my appetite was so large because I worked and trained hard and I was still growing. Those calories just burned up like nothing.

Well, the Pittsburgh Press somehow heard about this construction worker who was incredibly strong and who had this enormous appetite. One day when we weren't working, a Press reporter came over to my home and watched my Mom fix me breakfast. She made me scrambled eggs and besides that I ate a loaf of bread, a box of cereal and two quarts of milk. The reporter was astounded!

Then he tagged along with me to the gym. I did all kinds of lifting just to show him my strength. He went back and did a piece on me that appeared in the Sunday Roto section which everybody read. The article generated a lot of good publicity for me.

An early photo of me training.

Let me tell you about one experience I had while working at the Hilton Hotel. I was assigned to help out a a Swedish fellow named John Miller who was my partner that day. We were stripping a beam that had just received a concrete pour. I was down below the beam, prying with a crowbar. John crawled up on top of the beam and he started to hit it with a sledge hammer. I couldn't see him because those beams were two and a half feet wide, but I sure could hear him overhead, banging away with his hammer.

Before I could yell up to him, "Hey, what are you doing?", the beam came loose all of a sudden, hitting me solidly and knocking me down an elevator shaft. Talk about Laurel and Hardy. I fell two stories into some plywood planking that the elevator workers had just positioned and I came to a crashing halt on that. If those boys hadn't been working there and laid that plywood, I would have plunged nineteen stories down the shaft. Even so, I got shaken up pretty good and that set me back with my training.

Another time a foreman named Sal Williams came up to me to tell me about a business opportunity. He was well aware that I was the strongest man on the job site and he had seen me take on all comers at lunchtime in arm-wrestling. He wanted to know if I'd like to make an easy 50 dollars.

When you're an apprentice carpenter making about $20 a day then $50 sounds real good. I asked him what I had to do.

Apparently Sal had visited a carnival that was in Irwin just for the week. Irwin is a town just to the east of Pittsburgh. There he had seen a wrestling tent that featured a monkey who took on all challengers. The man who ran the exhibit bragged that nobody could last with his monkey for five minutes. Sal told the carnival operator that he knew a young fellow at work who definitely could last that long and more. So the two agreed to put up a $50 bet...monkey against me.

Sal told me that if I won I could keep the $50. He just wanted to see me whip this monkey. I asked Sal how big the monkey was. He said he hadn't stuck around to watch a match so he hadn't actually seen it, but he didn't think it was very big.

Sal really had a lot of confidence in me, betting so much money on my behalf against an opponent he hadn't even seen. But he added, that night we could catch the monkey on television. He had heard it was going to be featured on a local news show called Pitt Parade which aired around six o'clock. I told Sal I'd watch the show to size up this beast.

That night before I went to the gym, I flipped on KDKA for the news about the carnival. The camera showed a cage with this little shivering monkey in it, only about 18 inches high. That poor monkey looked like somebody's neglected pet. When l saw that, I said to myself you've got to be kidding. Who couldn't beat that chimp?

The next day I went up to Sal and I told him not to worry. I asked him how could he have any doubt that I wouldn't beat the monkey. I pledged to him that "Not only will I last five minutes, but I'll whip that monkey with both hands tied behind my back." So the match was on...to take place Friday evening after work.

Some of the guys at the site started kidding me, saying, "Bruno, don't you know those monkeys have sharp claws?"

I laughed, saying "I don't care. When I get my hands on that monkey, I show you all what will happen to those claws."

Since I was so full of confidence, everybody began to feel sorry for the monkey. The fellows told me to go easy on the poor little animal. After all, it wasn't the monkey who made the bet.

Finally, Friday rolled around and a huge group from work all climbed into their pickup trucks and cars and headed to the carnival in a caravan. When we arrived, Sal escorted me over to the tent and a heavy-set man met us, handing me a release to sign that stated the carnival was not responsible for anything that might happen to me and that I was entering into this match of my own free will.

As I was signing the paper, I noticed that the heavy guy's right hand only had a thumb on it. The other four fingers were missing. Not being a real man of the world at age twenty, I asked him what had happened.

He laughed and told me to be careful when I grabbed the monkey around the head. Even though the monkey had a muzzle on, the strap that held the device in place had a tendency to come loose...especially if I fooled with it in the wrong way.

The heavy guy kept hinting that the monkey had chewed off his fingers. I thought to myself, "Boy, that little animal must have some powerful jaws and teeth."

As I continued to talk with the heavy guy, I noticed there was a large cage, covered with canvas that was swaying back and forth...back and forth. I asked him, "What on earth is making all the ruckus in that cage?"

He chuckled and snorted, "That's your opponent, son." I couldn't believe it. "My opponent?" I thought, "How could that little monkey make that big cage rattle and shake?"

The heavy guy just looked at me and laughed. Soon the time came for me to enter the cage. All of my buddies from work packed the tent and were shouting encouragement to me as I waited. Then the canvas was drawn up and the monkey was unveiled. Nobody could believe it at first, especially me. The animal was huge and ugly...an orangutan! I stared at it for a second then shouted at the heavy guy over the crowd, "Hey, that's not the same monkey that was on TV!"

He rubbed his nose with his solitary thumb and snorted, "Who said you was gonna wrestle that monkey?" I took a deep breath and thought, "Oh, my God! What have I got myself into?" As I climbed inside and took my place at the opposite corner, I took a long look at the sucker. I almost froze because up close, the beast seemed even bigger...like King Kong or Mighty Joe Young. This was one ambitious looking animal..even with his muzzle

33

on. I stretched a bit, working my neck and shoulders loose, kicking at the straw on the cage floor. I was wearing a sweat suit and had on a pair of tights over that. I still wore my construction boots over sweatsocks. Remembering those warnings about the monkey claws, I had come prepared for combat. All the guys from work were screaming now, "Go get him, Bruno! Stomp that sucker!" That pumped me up and I started thinking that the match was going to be great! We got the signal to go and the battle was on. At first the orangutan just stood in his corner, hanging onto the bars and staring at me. I got the idea that he thought I was afraid since I wasn't making any moves toward him. All of a sudden, like lightning, he swung at me, his claws aiming for my face. Faster than I could imagine, he attacked, his feet like two pistons, pounding into me. He hung on me with his arms and then, boom, boom, boom with his feet into my sides. When I tried to duck, he was so swift and powerful that even when I tried to block his blows, he connected. Then as quick as he attacked, he darted away, taking up a position opposite me. He frowned at me, bewildered that I hadn't tumbled to the cage floor.

After that first flurry of blows, I had lost all fear of him because now I was angry and humiliated. I started to picture in my mind my amateur wrestling techniques. If only I could get behind him and force him to the floor, then I might have a chance to influence him. It was a good theory but as long as he continued to hang on the bars, I couldn't do anything.

I rushed him once, twice, three times with no luck. He darted away, leaving me grasping air. Then, on the fourth try I got behind him and was able to hook my arms around his chest. The crowd was going wild at this point.

At that time, I weighed around 265 pounds and was very strong, but when I moved to yank him down from the bars, he acted like he had a flea on his back. He swung around the cage with me hanging onto him for dear life. He always made sure to swing close to the bars so my back would scrape hard against the steel. After he circled the cage five or six times, I had to release my hold. I crashed to the floor, thinking my back was breaking.

The match went on, minute after minute and no matter what I would try, it was hopeless. The orangutan fought off all my best moves, then when I didn't expect it, he would let go of the cage with one paw and swing into me, sweeping me against the bars. I'd never wrestled anybody or anything as powerful as he was.

Fifteen minutes into the bout, I started to lose my vision. My eyes puffed up from the animal's steady pounding. I wasn't doing very well at all. We both took a couple of steps back and glared at each other. As he hung from his perch, I noticed that he was breathing heavily. Maybe I had started to wear him down.

I saw that his belly moved in and out as he sucked in air. It looked soft and I thought then that if I could connect with one hard shot to his mid-section, maybe I might have a chance to end this struggle before I went blind.

I rushed him and punched at his belly but I only half-connected. As soon as I did that, the carnival man who owned the orangutan stopped the fight, screaming that I was disqualified. He shouted that I cheated because I had thrown a punch in a wrestling match.

So even though that big, hairy beast could do everything he wanted, I had to play by the rules. At any rate we did win Sal William's $50 bet. I had lasted well over five minutes in the cage with this carnival Kong. And my buddies from work had something to talk about for quite a long time afterwards.

By the way, when I climbed down from the cage, all I had left on my body was my tights and my boots. The orangutan had shredded the rest of my clothes right off and I had blood all over my back and shoulders. My eyes were nearly shut from his attacks. As I headed out of the tent into the fresh air, I hoped that that would be the last time anybody would make a monkey out of me!

A dream come true was having my childhood idol
Primo Carnerra pose with me and mom in our house.

35

I worked with Turner Construction at the Hilton Hotel job site for nearly two years, from November of 1957 to late October of 1959. Throughout all that time, I continued with my weightlifting career.

In the summer of 1959, I won another important contest, a state power lifting championship and in the early part of Fall that year, Bob Prince asked me to come back on his show to talk about it. Bob remembered me from days as a novice lifter and wanted to follow with my latest accomplishments.

So in mid-October, I went on his show and he was very kind to me, giving me a big buildup. We chatted about how I had always loved wrestling, ever since I was a little boy in Italy and about how my childhood idol was the great Primo Carnerra, the Italian boxing king. I had dreamed about growing up to become as strong and capable a man as Primo Carnerra. Then Bob and I talked about how I went back and forth to Pitt and the Y to work out and how my life's ambition was to become a professional wrestler one day.

Little did I know that a man was watching me on KDKA's Bob Prince show that day who was to have an enormous impact on my life. His name was Rudy Miller and he was the local promoter, representing Capitol Wrestling in the eastern region. (Incidentally, Capitol Wrestling eventually evolved into the WWF.) As Capitol's agent, Rudy handled all their shows in the Pittsburgh area which included a television studio wrestling program

Rudy Miller, who I credit as discovering my wrestling talents.

that aired on Channel Eleven.

The next day, Rudy was at the Channel Eleven station and he happened to be jawing with a couple of friends of mine from High School...the Kartonis brothers. I was also in the Pennsylvania Air National Guard with these guys so they knew me pretty well.

The Kartonis brothers used to work the studio wrestling shows there, taking the jackets from the wrestlers in their corners before the matches would begin. Anyway, Rudy asked them if they knew this young kid from Pittsburgh named Bruno something who had been on the Bob Prince show the day before. He couldn't remember my last name.

They both knew who he was referring to right away and they chimed in that Rudy had seen Bruno Sammartino, a great guy and a tremendously strong wrestler. Rudy asked the brothers to get in touch with me and see if I would be willing to meet with him at the Channel Eleven studios.

So the Kartonis brothers contacted me to say that Rudy Miller, a professional wrestling promoter, was interested in meeting me. Of course, this was what I had been waiting for...a chance to meet somebody in the wrestling profession...an industry where I knew absolutely nobody.

The following week I drove over to Channel Eleven and made my way into the studio where live wrestling was broadcast. I saw the Kartonis brothers and walked over to join them. Then they introduced me to Rudy Miller and left the two of us alone.

Rudy started firing questions at me. "How much wrestling have you done in your life?" he wanted to know.

I told him that what I said on the Bob Prince show was true. I've loved wrestling ever since I was a little kid. Then I told him about my dedication to training and how I had walked every night after school to go and train at Pitt, wrestling with the college team. I mentioned how I continued to train at the Y, never letting up a minute.

He asked me to take off my jacket and shirt because he wanted to see what I looked like. Of course, thanks to my hard work and constant training, my physique did impress him.

Then he asked me a question that at the time I didn't quite understand. He said, "You say your name is Sammartino? You're Italian, right?"

"That's right."

"But you were born in America?"

I shook my head, "No, I was born in Italy."

Rudy's eyes opened a little wider. "Really? Do you speak Italian?"

I laughed, "Of course. I was born and raised there."

He clapped his hands together and said, "That's great!"

I didn't understand why he thought that was so "great". I mean I'm proud of my Italian heritage and I love to speak the language, but I just didn't get the connection.

In any case, Rudy asked me if I would like to travel to Washington, D.C. with him to meet a couple of other promoters, his partners Toots Mondt and Vince McMahon Sr. That made me stop and think for a second.

As I said before, this was in the fall of '59. I had just gotten married to my wife Carol on September 12th, after having gone together for nearly four years. As much as I wanted to say to Miller, "Yes, I'll go with you to Washington", I knew I couldn't do that immediately. I'd have to clear it with my foreman at work because I sure couldn't afford to lose my job just to go on an interview. And I knew I'd have to talk it over with my wife.

Carol and I had started out living with my parents on the second floor of their house and we really didn't have much of our own yet. Even though Carol had a job with Travelers Insurance as a typist, we still had to count on my salary as an apprentice carpenter to go with hers in order to make ends meet.

Rudy said to tell my foreman that I'd only be gone a couple of days and that this trip could be a very important step in my life. He said he doubted that I'd have any trouble and just get back to him when I got the okay. So I agreed to ask my foreman for permission to leave the job site for a few days to go meet Mondt and McMahon.

Frankly, I was more than a little nervous about it since my foreman, Ralph Trapazano from Philadelphia, had been very good to me. Thanks to him, I had finally started to make a decent wage at the Hilton Hotel site after being on the job there for two straight years and he had seen to it that my job responsibilites had started to grow.

Early on, Mister Trapazano had come to me and said, "I heard from the business agent that all people ever use you for is bull-work. To load, unload, dig, carry? Is that right?"

I said that was true.

"Well, you're an apprentice carpenter, right?"

I said "Yeah, that's right. And I'm getting a little worried about my apprenticeship running out without ever being allowed to handle a hammer or a saw." I added, "How am I supposed to get work later when I don't know anything about carpentry?"

Mister Trapazano shook his head and said, "Well, Bruno, just listen to me. You're going to be an apprentice carpenter over here in my crew and if anybody tells you to do something that you're not supposed to do, then tell me about it. You know the apprentice rules, don't you?"

I said, "Yes, sir!"

There were a lot of people working on the Hilton Hotel job. I couldn't believe that anybody there really cared about me like Mister Trapazano did. In the past, if anybody needed bull-work, they'd say "Go get Bruno" and anytime they needed somebody to lift, they'd say "Go get Bruno." Mister Trapazano changed all that so naturally I didn't want to do anything to offend him or to show him I wasn't appreciative of everything he had done for me.

The next day when I went back to work, I was leery about even asking him. Here he was, giving me all that overtime and now I wanted to take off for Washington, D.C.

Finally, I went over to him in the middle of the morning and said, "Mister Trapazano, may I have a few words with you?"

He smiled and said, "Bruno, I've told you a hundred times to call me Ralph."

I said, "I'm sorry, Mister Trapazano, but that's the way I was raised. You're my boss and I owe you respect so that's why I call you Mister Trapazano."

"Okay," he said, "What's on your mind, Bruno?" So I told him how ever since I came from Italy when I was fifteen, I had a dream. It was a dream that I never even told my parents about because I didn't want to be laughed at or thought crazy. My dream was someday to become a professional wrestler and it was to this goal that I had trained so hard all of my life. I told Mister Trapazano that in fact when I left work, l would go to the gym for four hours every night and work out, day in and day out, week after week, weightlifting, wrestling and waiting for my chance to fulfill my dream.

Then with a big lump in my throat, I said that I had met a promoter by the name of Rudy Miller who wanted me to go to Washington, D.C. for two days so that two other promoters could take a close look at me. I said that if my absence would cause any problems on the job, I would tell Miller just to forget it.

Mister Trapazano waited until I was finished, smiled again and said, "Bruno, if things work out for you and you aren't coming back, just let me know. As far as I'm concerned, you have my permission to go."

I was overjoyed. After work, I went back to the television station and luckily Rudy Miller was still there. I told him that my boss had agreed to let me go. Then I stopped dead. "I don't have any money for a plane ticket. Maybe I'll have to drive there."

Miller said, "Don't worry about that stuff." He reached into his pocket, pulled out a big wad of bills and peeled off five one hundred dollar bills for me. He said, "Use this to buy your plane tickets and use the rest for any other expenses you might have on the way. It should be plenty but don't worry. I'll be meeting you down there too and I can give you more if you run out of cash."

Five hundred dollars to me was a fortune. Especially since I was making twenty dollars a day as an apprentice carpenter.

When I went home and told my wife Carol that a wrestling promoter had given me $500 to go to Washington, she asked me, "Bruno, why can't you get wrestling out of your head? Why don't you just forget it? You're going to be a carpenter. With me working for Travelers, we'll have enough."

I said to her, "Honey, I can't go through my life without giving my dream a shot. I have to try."

Finally, she was very unhappy about it, but knowing how much it meant to me, she said that I should go.

So in mid-November I went to the address in D.C. that Rudy Miller had given me and I met Toots Mondt, an old-time wrestler who had become a promoter, and his partner, Vince McMahon, Sr. We all sat down in their office and they started to ask me about my wrestling.

When did I start? How much experience did I have? Am I really Italian? Then they did something that threw me.

Pittsburgh Promoter, Joseph (Toots) Mondt.

Vince McMahon, President of Capitol Wrestling in D.C.

McMahon picked up the phone and called someone they knew that spoke Italian and he asked me to speak to this man. I got on the phone and the man says to me, "Bon journo" and he asked me several questions in Italian such as "How long have you been in this country?" and "How much do you like wrestling?". I answered all of his questions in Italian.

After we had spoken for a while, the mysterious man asked me if I would put McMahon back on the line. He then verified to the promoter that yes, Bruno Sammartino could spoke fluent Italian.

What I didn't understand at the time but realized later was that if you were a foreigner in wrestling, it was a tremendous drawing card. The promoters loved to pit different wrestlers from different backgrounds against each other.

With my Italian heritage checked out, Mondt and McMahon had me stay over that night. They even took me out to dinner.

Next day, bright and early, I was taken to a gymnasium in the area where a ring was set up. A couple of pro wrestlers were working out when we arrived so the two promoters asked me to see what I could do with one of them.

I climbed into the ring with the first man and went into my amateur stance. When he came at me, I immediately tried to get behind him, but he blocked me easily. I tried to get behind him a second time and again he blocked my move. Then I faked the move behind, went for his leg and I took him down, riding him onto the mat. We went at each other for a while and to be honest, I impressed this pro somewhat.

Then the promoters had the second pro come in and I worked out with him, too. He tried different professional moves on me and I countered very well. You know, despite what people think, there are a number of professional moves that are unfamiliar and therefore tough for amateur wrestlers. That's because amateur wrestlers aren't taught about submission wrestling. That's certainly not the case in professional wrestling where there are many pros who have mastered the art of total dominance of an opponent.

What helped me get through this tryout, even though I was being thrown moves that I'd never seen before, was my power, my strength and my quickness. Either I wouldn't get caught in them in the first place or I'd just bull my way out if I did.

After the two workout sessions were over and I had showered and toweled off, the promoters came back to me and said that I had impressed them. They wanted me to stay for a month and train with pros like the ones I had just wrestled with before they turned me pro. At first I didn't know what to say.

I blurted out that "I have to go back to Pittsburgh because I told my boss and my wife I'd only be gone two days." Then it hit me. I said, "But wait a minute. Does this mean you think I'm good enough to compete professionally?"

Both Mondt and McMahon nodded and said, "Yes, Bruno. Absolutely!" Then McMahon added, "Bruno go back to Pittsburgh and tell them you're quitting your job. You're going to be a professional wrestler. We'll have the contract waiting for you when you get back."

I said, "Okay. Fantastic! I'll go back and make the arrangements...talk to my boss and discuss it with my wife."

And so I went back home and told my wife Carol about what had happened to me. But instead of us dancing for joy, she nearly couldn't hold back her tears. We'd gotten married less than two months ago and here I was talking about quitting the job I'd held for nearly two years to become a professional wrestler. It just didn't make sense to her.

The next day when I returned to work, I immediately went to see Mister Trapazano and I told him everything that had happened. It didn't take him long to give me an answer.

He said, "Bruno, you don't really belong here in construction. You're a big, strong guy with a lot of talent. I think everybody's here for a purpose and I don't think that yours was to be a carpenter. Go ahead and follow your dream. I'll be watching in the newspapers to see what happens to you."

Grateful for his understanding and his blessing, I thanked him for the two years of steady work he'd given me and then I left for home. Then I told my wife that I had quit my construction job...and then I told her parents.

They were surprised by what I had done especially since I had never spoken to them about my plans. I told them that I didn't want anybody to think I was crazy but I had always had this dream. I told them that I had to go chase it now because otherwise I might never have another chance to see if I was good enough or not. And they understood. Then privately, my in-laws told me not to worry about Carol. They said that they would take care of her and help her to understand what her husband was doing.

When I told my own parents what I had decided to do, they were definitely not in favor. My mother was scared about what would happen to her son, leaving home and going into a profession where I could be hurt badly. My father didn't see wrestling as a respectable business for a family man to be in. They both were disappointed with my choice, but to their great credit, they didn't fight me on it.

Everyone knew that I had to find out if I could make it as a pro. And I knew that everything I'd ever worked for was at stake.

MY PROFESSIONAL CAREER BEGINS

I left for Washington, D.C. as soon as I could make travel arrangements. When I got there, I trained and trained hard. Every morning I would work out with professional wrestlers who were signed on with the Capitol card, then at night, when the pros would scatter to their scheduled bouts, I'd go to the local YMCA to pump iron.

I maintained that routine for a whole month and then it came time to turn pro. Mondt and McMahon handed me my contract and asked me to sign on the dotted line.

I had never seen a contract before and I didn't realize that I should have had an attorney look it over. At first glance, it seemed really simple to me. I was to be paid $250 a week salary and anything that I earned over that from boxoffice proceeds would be split 50-50 with them.

Now I'd never traveled much and not knowing how these things were handled, I asked them if the $250 that I was getting in salary was going to be enough to cover my expenses. I said that I didn't know what it would cost for hotels and meals or for transportation.

McMahon gave me his assurance that I would travel mostly by car and that there would always be someone driving with me to share costs. He told me that I'd be wrestling mainly between New York, New Jersey, Connecticut and Pennsylvania.

"Okay," I said, "But really, I'm not so sure that $250 is going to be enough to live on and send money home to my wife."

McMahon told me, "Don't worry, Bruno. The $250 is only for your expenses. That's your guarantee. The bulk of your money is going to come from the 50-50 split."

What he said seemed to make sense. I felt good about it and thought, "Okay, I'm 24 years old. I can take care of myself. So I signed it.

When I called home to my wife and explained the deal to her, she said that she really didn't understand too much about it. It was obvious that she still didn't like the idea of me going off to become a professional wrestler. To her the money wasn't all that important. She just wanted to know when I'd be home and how often.

From the beginning, life was rough. For whatever reason, that $250 guarantee was all that I was getting. I never did get anymore than that $250. I can laugh about it now, years later, but believe me, it was serious business at the time.

Yes, it was true that I was driving to all my matches, but as it turned out, it was usually with one of Capitol's agents...and he would actually charge me transportation costs to make these trips. Then too I was paying for my hotel rooms plus trying to curb my enormous appetite out of that $250.

So I was supposed to make my extra money from gate receipts everywhere I wrestled, right? After a while I was wrestling in Madison Square Garden and even then there weren't any gate receipts to split. That's what I was told, anyway.

The problem turned out to be that there had never been any predetermined amount specified as far as indicating what percentage of each match I would receive. The contract stated that I'd share in profits but not when the profits would begin.

Capitol just gave me whatever they felt like, whenever they felt like it. And it was never much.

I was quite a bashful person in those days and for a while I just kept quiet. I didn't want to stir things up. But after a while enough was enough and I finally went to Rudy Miller to ask him some tough questions. "Rudy," I wanted to know. "When am I going to make some decent money?"

Rudy was patient with me. He said, "Bruno, you're new to this business. It's going to take a while to get yourself established. For now, you're going to have to manage your money carefully."

I said, "All I do with my money is pay bills. Sometimes after paying for my room, there's not even enough money left to buy food...and Rudy, I stay at the cheapest hotels I can find." What I didn't tell him was that with my pennypinching, I managed to send Carol about $75 of my guarantee every month.

He looked at me, smiled and said, "Bruno, you just got to be patient. Things will turn around for you real soon. You can depend on it."

I was starting to have second thoughts about everything. Now I wanted to know exactly what was going on. I made a few inquiries and in a short time I found out that there was more to professional wrestling than meets the eye.

A New York promoter by the name of Kola Kwariani kept coming up in conversation. It seemed that Kwariani had made a deal some time ago with Vince McMahon and Toots Mondt to combine the entire Northeast wrestling territory. Even though Kwariani was based in the Big Apple and McMahon and Mondt were based in Washington, D.C., they were actually partners in the running of the whole Northeast game.

Now there was a feud going on...one that was shaking this partnership to pieces. The three promoters had decided to split the territory in half. Kola Kwariani was to receive New York, New Jersey and parts of Connecticut.

McMahon was going off on his own, taking Washington, Maryland, Pennsylvania and what was left of Connecticut.

Where did Rudy Miller and Toots Mondt fit in then? They sided with Kwariani in the feud.

Wrestlers were caught in the middle of the fight. The promoters were playing a tug of war and each of us pros had to decide which camp we would wrestle for from this point on.

I knew that I was under contract with Vince McMahon. I also knew that I was just barely scraping by on the money McMahon paid me. Miller and Mondt were pushing me to Kwariani, telling me that McMahon didn't have any real development plans for my career but Kwariani wanted me and Tony Rocca to join up as tag team partners.

I struggled with my decision then finally agreed to go with Kola Kwariani. When I told Miller this, Rudy said that he and Toots would take care of telling McMahon the news. They said I was to report immediately to Kwariani's office at the Holland Hotel on 42nd Street in New York.

I flew up and went to meet the man. Kwariani, as it turned out, had been a powerful wrestler in his day. He wrestled as an amateur in his native Russia then came to America to become a pro here.

Now as an old man, he had become a promoter in the sport he loved best. He spoke to me in a thick accent almost too difficult to understand. "Bruno" he said, "You will wrestle for me and you will become a big star some day. All you have to do is just listen to me, Kola Kwariani, and do exactly what I say."

I answered quickly, "Yes, sir. Whatever you say." He impressed me as someone who knew the business and was an honorable man. So I began to wrestle for Kwariani in what turned out to be a very turbulent period in my career.

Shortly after I joined Kwariani's ranks, he got broadsided by the State Athletic Commission. This was the official wrestling association that had jurisdiction over him and they had just become very tough on violence. They began to enforce restrictions on what may or may not appear on television and at live appearances in arenas. In other words, they took the bite out of what we could or couldn't do as wrestlers.

Down in Washington, D.C. it was a different story. McMahon had no Commission to contend with so he was free to be as wild as he wanted to be. This translated into big box office. McMahon started to win the war for gate attendance as the fans flocked to the more exciting and exuberant matches he promoted.

Kwariani was in trouble. Other local promoters were abandoning the old

Russian and calling for McMahon's services.

Finally, Kwariani brought me into his office and told me that if things continued the way they were that I should try to find another promoter who could handle me better than he could. He just said that his hands were tied by the Commission and even though they were ruining his business, there was nothing he could do.

I went back to where I was staying and called Rudy Miller, telling him what was happening and asking him and Toots Mondt for their guidance. Where could I find another promoter who could take over for Kwariani

Miller was blunt. He blamed Kwariani for all my problems. He told me that the best thing to do would be for him to talk to Vince McMahon to see if Vince would take me back. Miller said he wasn't so sure that this would work because he knew McMahon to be a man who held grudges.

Well, McMahon did agree to let me return to his fold but he certainly didn't have the most noble intentions. He conducted a war of nerves with me and he commanded the artillery.

Here's what he would do. Let's say he'd run two shows in his territory on one particular night. One show might be at the Civic Arena in Pittsburgh which is a large facility. The other show would be held in New Castle, a small town in Northeastern Pennsylvania. Guess who would end up going to New Castle to appear in the opening match?

As lightweight as those bookings were, McMahon would only give me one or two of them a week. The payoffs would be $20 or $25. I just couldn't survive on that kind of money, especially since my wife Carol had given birth to our first child, our son David, who was born on September 29, 1960. I now had ever greater responsibilities to my family. I'd been a professional wrestler for close to a year and was just barely getting by. What was I to do?

I told Rudy Miller what was going on and he said there was nothing he and Toots could do for me. That's just the way McMahon operated. When you were on McMahon's List, you stayed there.

Rudy suggested that I might be better off with another promoter in another territory. I told him I didn't know any other promoters. Rudy volunteered to phone around and see what he could dig up, promising not to let the word get around that I was looking for an escape route from McMahon.

Miller called Detroit promoter Johnny Doyle who said he could use an Italian name on his cards. I agreed to go with Doyle, thinking by now that anything which would take me out from under McMahon would be a good move.

I went to McMahon, told him that I was leaving after I finished my last two bookings and did just that. I wrestled two more matches then packed my bags for San Francisco.

That's right...San Francisco, not Detroit. While I was fulfilling my final obligations with McMahon, Johnny Doyle was already hard at work on my behalf. Doyle and a San Francisco promoter, Roy Shars, were collaborating with their first show at the Cow Palace. Because there were many Italians in the Bay Area, Doyle worked out a deal with Shars to have me booked there.

Once I arrived, I wrestled on their card then stayed over to wrestle in some other local matches that Doyle had booked me for. While I was getting ready to do a TV match one night, a couple of guys from the State Athletic Commission cornered me before I went on. They told me that I couldn't wrestle that night...that I had been suspended. I was astonished. "Suspended? What are you talking about?"

They were arrogant, smirking. One guy just said, "In plain English, Bruno...you can't wrestle. Suspended."

I stammered, "Why am I suspended? What have I done?" "You mean you don't know what you've done? Or where you did it?" he said, turning away. "I have no idea," I said. "That's too bad, Bruno. Just don't try crawling through the ropes tonight or any night. You're through." The two men left me standing there, shaking my head. I rushed over to Doyle and cornered him, asking "Why had I been suspended? What had I done?" Doyle shrugged, saying "Well, kid...I don't know what you did. I'll see if I can find out. It took Doyle two days to get back to me. I was frantic, upset...an innocent man accused of an unknown crime...and nobody was talking. Doyle told me on the phone nothing that I didn't know already. He said, "All I know is that you're suspended. They won't let you wrestle in this territory anymore. I don't know what to tell you. Maybe you need to find yourself another place to go. There's a guy I know in Indianapolis...Jim Barnett. Let me give him a call. See if he can fit you in on a couple of matches." After a few quick phone calls back and forth, I was on my way back East to Indianapolis. I had just enough money to get there and when I arrived, it was the same old song on the jukebox. Just as McMahon had done to me, Barnett was only giving me a $25 payroll for my matches. I got the small stuff and that was it. I couldn't even make enough money to feed myself or stay in a decent motel room, much less take care of my wife and baby boy. Out of my $25 payoff, I would keep only $10 for myself and send $15 home to my wife. I wouldn't check into a hotel because where could you stay for $10? I'd go to a delicatessen, buy a loaf of bread and some cheap cold cuts and I'd find a place to go and eat my meal, drinking gallons of water to wash it all down. Then instead of checking into a hotel, I'd go into the lobby of a nice place and sit in a sofa or chair, pretending to be waiting for someone. I'd spend as much time as I could in that chair or sofa until I was chased out. I was becoming very despondent. So I tried to see the promoter, this Jim Barnett to get him to tell me why I was only wrestling once or twice a week and why I was making such little money. I went to his office but Barnett wouldn't see me. Nobody in his office could help me either. I decided to make my way back home to Pittsburgh. That was it. I had no money and I was whipped. I couldn't figure out what the suspension had been all about. I had been judged and found guilty with my sentence being exile from the profession I loved so very much.

UNRAVELING THE MYSTERY

I hitchhiked back to Pittsburgh. I had never hitchhiked in my life because I just was not that kind of person. I was very shy and bashful. But I had no money and no choice.

I made it home completely exhausted. I was depressed and confused. On the one hand, it was wonderful to be with my wife and family again but how was I to support them now?

I called one of the local contractors that I had worked for several years ago, Mister Henry Busey, and talked to him about returning to construction work. He agreed to hire me back as a laborer for a while.

While I had been gone, the wrestling game in Pittsburgh had taken on a different look. Toots Mondt had started promotions in Pittsburgh and had a guy named Ace Freeman running the operation for him. But looks are deceiving at times because the Pittsburgh territory was still under Capitol Wrestling and McMahon still held everyone on a short leash.

When Toots heard that I was back home working construction, he contacted me and asked if we could meet. When I went to see him, the first thing I wanted to know was if he knew anything about my suspension. I told him I hadn't been able to learn anything and because I had a wife and baby to support, I had to come home and find a job to feed my family.

Toots got straight to the point. ''Look, I know this suspension has been rough on you but things can be worked out. First, let me ask you if you'd like to wrestle here in Pittsburgh?''

Here I am all smiles with McMahon, Mondt, and Bill Cardille.

49

"Sure," I said, "But how much wrestling could there be here?" Toots thought maybe three days a week minimum. I told him that I didn't think that I'd make enough money to take care of my family just wrestling three days a week. Toots leaned back in his chair and said, "Bruno, let me tell you something. If you want me to, I can patch things up between you and McMahon. If that happens, then you'll be back on the full circuit." "What about the suspension?" I wanted to know. "That can be taken care of too. All you got to do is just give the word." Once more I went to the well. I told Toots that I'd take another chance on him if he could do all the things he said he could. And I knew that even though my dream had become tarnished, it was still alive in my heart. So I started wrestling again for Toots...and I found myself back in New Castle, Pennsylvania with an $11 payoff. Then I went to McKeesport and was paid $16. Another match I was paid $7. I was getting very angry again. I went back to Mondt and laid it out for him. "These matches just don't make it. You've got to do better for me."

A tough match in New Castle, PA brings me only $11.00!

Toots told me to hold on. "I spoke to Vince earlier and we're going to get that suspension fixed for you. That means you can start wrestling all over the territory again."

"Does that mean that you know why I was suspended?" I asked. "And where my violation was supposed to have taken place?"

"It was in Baltimore, Maryland. You were scheduled for a match and you never showed up."

I cut in, "That's impossible. I've always made all my bookings...no matter what."

Toots just shook his head "Don't question it. The main thing is to get it cleared up. That's what counts." He reached into his wallet and handed me a wad of cash. "Here's money to fly to Baltimore. McMahon will meet you there and take you to the Commission. Okay?"

Toots was right. Clearing up the suspension was what counted. I agreed to go as soon as possible.

I met McMahon in Baltimore and this was the first time I had talked to him since I had left him for Johnny Doyle. He told me that we would meet with the State Athletic Commission right away and that he wanted to make one thing clear. He'd do all the talking and I was to keep my mouth shut.

"Is that clear, Bruno?" McMahon asked me. I nodded, "Sure, I understood. I won t say a word." McMahon and I drove right over to the Commission office and were ushered into a large room and all the Commissioners and Deputy Commissioners were sitting at the table just staring at me. I just sat there like a dummy, keeping my mouth shut. The Head Commissioner snapped at me, "For what you did, Sammartino, we should suspend you for life." McMahon glared over at me, giving me the sign not to say anything back to the Head Commissioner. I'm still thinking to myself, "What is this guy talking about?" The Head Commissioner went on, "Now because Vince McMahon has interceded on your behalf and has come to this Commission personally, we are going to respect his request to lift your suspension. In addition, we are only going to fine you $500. As soon as the fine is paid, the suspension is no longer in effect. McMahon motioned me not to speak again, then he said, "Thank you, Mister Commissioner, for your consideration. We accept your decision."

"Let me tell you one more thing, Sammartino. If you ever do anything like this again," the Commissioner added, "you will be banned from professional wrestling for life!" So saying this, the Head Commissioner adjourned the meeting...a meeting in which I didn't say one word. Before we left their offices, McMahon had paid my $500 fine and then told me in the hall, "When you start working for me again, that $500 will be coming from your pay. Understand?''

"All right. Fine. But still nobody said officially why I was suspended." I just wanted to know the truth.

McMahon glared at me. "Bruno, what's done is done. Just get your butt back to Pittsburgh and do your shows. Toots'll tell you about your bookings from now on."

So I went back home...and started wrestling again. What I quickly found out was that money was still as scarce as ever for me. Finally, when I worked Madison Square Garden and received a paltry $50 for my efforts, I made my mind up. I just couldn't go on with my life this way. Once again I became a very bitter guy. Very bitter!

Then I found out the story behind my suspension. I was enraged! Let me tell you what had happened.

As I mentioned before, McMahon held a grudge against me for leaving

An early studio pose. My ears still looked normal!

him and going with Kola Kwariani. When things didn't work out with

Kwariani, McMahon had reluctantly agreed to put me back on his roster. The catch was that I only worked the curtain opener. He made me into the opening match against the worst of opponents and always in the smallest club. Then even these miserable dates would be spread so far apart that I couldn't make a living.

That was when I went to Rudy Miller and appealed to him. Could he help me out with McMahon? And that was when Rudy contacted Johnny Doyle from Detroit and I ended up in San Francisco, wrestling for Doyle and Roy Shars.

It was at that point that McMahon decided that Capitol Wrestling was going to teach this "young wop" a lesson. Yes, that's how they referred to Italians in those days. "Wop" or "ginnie" or "dago."

What McMahon did was book me in Baltimore for a match and then just didn't tell me about it. When I finished my two remaining matches in Pittsburgh and left for the Coast, to the best of my knowledge I was through with Capitol.

Of course, I didn't show up in Baltimore. I didn't know about the match. McMahon then contacted the Commission and asked them to take disciplinary against this punk Sammartino.

I can just imagine McMahon on the phone to them, saying, "I've had nothing but trouble with this kid. We've got to teach him a lesson. Who does he think he is...not showing up for a scheduled match?" Yes, I can just imagine. And I'm sure the Commission listened well to what McMahon had to say...especially since they were being taken care of by the promoters.

I don't know what the Commission members are like today, but in those days, as far as I'm concerned, they were corrupt, corrupt, corrupt. Look at my suspension. It was an illegal suspension. Before they can suspend you, you must be given a hearing where evidence is presented. You have to be given a chance to defend yourself against your accusers. You can't just be blackballed like I was. They had suspended me with no explanation...no reason. I never even received a notice, detailing the charges. I was never given the chance to appeal.

So why did McMahon tell me not to question the suspension? Because if I had, I would have found out that it was McMahon who had masterminded it all along.

What McMahon didn't count on was that this "young wop" did find out how he had been deceived. I began to look for an escape route once more...a way to pull myself loose from McMahon's web.

As things often happen, when you decide to make a move in a certain direction, events come together to allow you to do it. I found out that there was a promoter with a very good reputation who worked out of Toronto, Canada. His name was Frank Tunney and he was having trouble getting the crowds to come to his shows. I contacted Tunney early in 1961 and told him that I was an Italian wrestler, who could speak the language fluently. I told him that I understood that there were over 500,000 Italians living in Toronto and that I felt if he would give me the opportunity, I could draw those people in to see me wrestle. After thinking it over, Tunney quickly agreed. I asked him only one favor. I told him, "No one must know that I am coming to Canada. When I arrive, I'll be happy to explain to you the reason for my secrecy but until I do, you must not tell a soul."

Tunney said that was all right with him, then asked me when I could be in Toronto.

I explained to him that I still had a few dates left with Capitol which I had to fulfill. We figured out a starting date for me and that was that. I was on my way to Canada.

By now, I was growing up....getting a little smarter. I contacted McMahon and verified all the dates for my bookings. Then I told him not to book me for any more matches. He wanted to know what the hell was going on...again.

I told him calmly that I was fulfilling all my obligations with him and that I was leaving Capitol. I wouldn't say where. That was my business.

I didn't trust McMahon one tiny bit. To cover myself against anything like what had happened the last time, I sent certified letters to each and every State Athletic Commission office in the United States of America, saying that I was booked with Capitol Wrestling until a certain date. If I should be booked by them after this date, it would be done without my agreement or permission. I added that I would be employed by another concern and that Capitol no longer represented me.

This time, I had all of those certified receipts in hand. No one was going to level me with false accusations...not again.

My decision to wrestle in Canada drew a lot of fire and generated considerable anger from Capitol. It didn't take long for McMahon and Mondt to find out that I was in Toronto and to apply the pressure once more...this time on Frank Tunney.

My first few months up North were as bad as back home. I wasn't making much money. At least Tunney booked me six nights as week and I wrestled as much as I could. I would find cheap places to hole up in and then send as much as I could back home to Carol.

I had to face facts. We were in deep debt and getting deeper. Medical bills were piling up, stemming from physical problems that Carol had to face after the birth of our son David. Her problems were so bad that our doctor told us we weren't to have any more children until Carol had recovered. In the meantime, the stack of bills rose higher and higher.

To make extra money I agreed to be booked for every possible appearance and I began a campaign to help my own situation. I became my own public relations man.

I contacted the Italian press in Toronto, told them where I was from and spoke to them in Italian. I told them that I could perform feats that not many in the world could accomplish and I invited the reporters to the gym to watch me train. They came and saw me doing a 570 pound bench press, a world record lift in those days. I squatted over 700 pounds. As I was lifting these enormous weights, the photographers started to snap pictures like crazy, Soon they ran stories in their newspapers about me, calling me "The Italian Superman."

I used the same tactic with Italian radio, informing them about my background then appearing on the air, talking about the old country. I told the audiences all about coming over here and about how happy I was to be wrestling in Toronto.

I was doing something that no one had ever done for me before...

I found happier times in Toronto.

promoting Bruno Sammartino. And it worked. The crowds started to come to see Bruno...one of Italy's Favorite Sons.

A few months after I had started wrestling for Tunney and business was picking up, he invited me to dinner...a great Chinese restaurant in the heart of Toronto. Frank liked to have a few drinks now and again and this night he told me things that if sober, he might not have said.

Frank was a man about 5'10", in his late forties when I met him. He had grayish hair that he combed straight back with a part in the side. He wore glasses, had a little pot belly, always had a cigar in his mouth and a smile that wrapped around it.

That night he said, "Bruno, I'm very glad that I don't let people influence me very easily. I could have made a bad mistake about you had I listened. And you wouldn't have deserved it. Now that I know you better I am so glad I took a chance on you." I asked him what he was talking about? Frank told me, "When you first arrived here in Toronto, I got a phone call about you."

"A phone call? From who?"

"That's not important. What's important is that they told me you're nothing but a troublemaker and that I should let you go immediately."

"I think I can guess who made that call," I said.

"They told me I'd have nothing but problems with Sammartino and that you weren't worth the time of day. I told Vince that if he was correct in his judgement, then I'd just tell you to pack your bags and go back to Pittsburgh."

I nodded, Vince McMahon. I see. What else did you say?"

Tunney took another sip of his drink. "You know Bruno, I had to take a chance on you. Let's face it. Things hadn't been going well for me until you showed up. A half a million Italians can't be all wrong. The crowds are getting bigger thanks to you. I want you to know that I appreciate everything you're doing for me. If you want to make Toronto your home, you can stay with me as long as you want."

For the first time in I don't know how long, I felt good. Tunney's words picked me up. I felt like I had a shot...like I was going to get a decent chance.

I felt good not only for me but for my wife. You know, even as bad as life was for us at the time, she had never complained. I realized that I wasn't the provider for her that I wanted to be. Knowing that I wasn't brought me very low many times.

Because I had gone through such difficulty during the war and afterward, the last thing in the world I wanted to do was to bring somebody into my life and instead of making life better for them, make it worse.

My father-in-law was an accountant so I guess you'd call Carol's family middle-class. Not poor by any means. Although my father-in-law didn't make that much money, he did own his own home and drove his own car which he traded in every two or three years. And their family used to go to Atlantic City or to Florida for vacation every year.

Carol had known a life that wasn't as bad as the one she was living with me. But never once did she chastise me. She'd never say, "See how things have worked out. I asked you not to try and do what you're doing. Now look what has happened to us."

After my dinner with Tunney, I telephoned Carol and told her that I thought I was about to get my shot. And that I had worked out an arrangement with Tunney so I could get home every two weeks for one day. This made her very happy...knowing that we could be together at least one or two days a month.

So right on schedule, I'd wrestle in Wellant, Ontario on Saturday, then rush to catch a bus to Buffalo, New York. I'd jump on the midnight bus from Buffalo and arrive in Pittsburgh by mid-morning on Sunday. It seemed like that bus stopped every other mile.

Then I'd spend a day at home with my family and early Monday morning I'd hurry out to the Pittsburgh airport and catch a flight back to Buf-

I began to make a name for myself in Canada.

falo. In Buffalo, I'd bus to wherever I was scheduled to wrestle that night which was usually Hamilton. Tunney would always try to book me close to Buffalo on Monday nights to accommodate my trips back home.

I began to make a name for myself in Canada.

My career was starting to build momentum. All throughout Canada, the word was that Toronto was dead for wrestling until the powerful young Italian guy had rode into town. All of a sudden, Frank Tunney was getting requests from Winnipeg and Vancouver from other promoters. Could we use Bruno for our show here? Could you spare him next week in Montreal?

Tunney would readily allow me to travel to Vancouver, to Calgary and to Montreal to wrestle there for other promoters. Thanks to this, my name was getting recognition throughout Canada.

I have to say here that Frank was one of the most decent persons I've known in my life. I don't really know if there are any other promoters who could compare with him. He was simply a nice man who was always willing to listen to the other guy and help out when he could. God rest his soul now for he died in 1983 at the age of 70. I'll certainly never forget him and what he did for me.

While all this was going on in Canada, meanwhile in New York, wrestling was in bad shape. Buddy Rogers was the world's champion and the crowds were going from bad to worse. When Capitol heard that Bruno Sammartino was having lots of success up North, they decided to try and lure me back.

Around the end of 1962, Ace Freeman, Capitol's man in charge in the Pittsburgh area, gave me a call while I was at home visiting my family. He said Vince McMahon wanted to talk to me.

I told Ace, "If Vince wants to talk to me, let him call me directly." I wasn't going to call him, not after everything that had happened between us.

I went back to Canada the next day, wrestled for two weeks straight and came back to Pittsburgh again. This time McMahon called me at home personally.

He said "Bruno, I understand you're doing all right in Canada. Congratulations."

"Vince," I said, "I thank God that I have met a man who believes in me. Yes, I am doing well. I'm being treated well and I am very happy in Canada."

"But Bruno, you know and I know that New York is the big time. That's where all the action is."

I paused a second then said, "Vince, I understand that New York isn't doing too good right now. In fact, I hear it stinks."

Vince sputtered, "Yeah? Who told you that?"

"Oh, a couple of wrestlers that I met in Canada had come up there because they said they couldn't make a living in New York," I said.

"Look," Vince interrupted, "Maybe things were down a few months ago, but right now it's different. Let me say three words to you...Madison Square Garden. If we do the right thing by you...you know, promote the hell out of you..."

That's where I stopped him. "Vince, I was there for you once before. Why wasn't the right thing done then?"

He jumped in again, "One thing you have to learn in this business is to bury the hatchet. Mistakes were made. Maybe I made some. Maybe you made some. You have to forget about the past and go with the future."

We argued back and forth. I had been in Canada now for about a year and a half. I told McMahon that I still didn't think that I was anywhere near wearing out my welcome there. I was doing well and I had a feeling that my good luck was going to continue.

"Vince, just listen to what has happened. I have offers from St. Louis. The National Wrestling Alliance wants me to go there. I got calls from Minneapolis...from California. I got a trip lined up to go to Japan."

And we talked, on and on over a period of a couple weeks. McMahon kept hitting me with his logic...New York was the big time. Why wasn't I there getting my share?

Finally, McMahon convinced me of one thing. If I was given the proper opportunity, I believed I could make it in New York. But it had to be on my own terms.

In my 18 months in Canada, I had learned...about success and about promotion. I knew that if I returned to Madison Square Garden that it would have to be for the biggest prize...the heavyweight championship.

So I told McMahon that I would return to New York only if he put me in the ring with Buddy Rogers for the title. This would be the perfect scenario for me...taking on Buddy Rogers, a man that I disliked immensely.

From the time I turned pro in 1959 until I took him on for the championship, I think I wrestled Nature Boy Buddy Rogers about a half dozen times. There were never any clear victories on either side. When he won over me, once both of us were outside the ring and he got back in, beating the count of ten before I could respond. Another time he knocked me out of the ring and I was unable to climb back before being counted out.

I defeated him in a couple of bouts, too. Once, when he had just won the championship belt, I gave him all he could handle in a match that was held in Pittsburgh. I was the clear winner and when the judges came to give me the belt, Buddy Rogers was still on the mat, holding his groin and accusing me of foul play.

I refused to take the belt under those circumstances. I didn't want any part of a championship where my honesty might be criticized fairly or unfairly. So I passed. I got the victory but I didn't get the title.

All together in our six matches before the title bout, we were dead even in wins and losses. He was a tough opponent, no question about that. I was never able to pin him or make him submit during those six matches, except for the one match in which he claimed a foul. I had wrestled him in two tag team matches, where it was Rocco and me against Rogers and Valentine. We defeated the Rogers team twice but it didn't count for anything but the glory because they were both non-title bouts.

In my heart, I held no love for Buddy Rogers. Actually I wasn't the only one to feel that way. He was a hated man for what he had done in the ring. He had hurt quite a few wrestlers, taking great pride in doing so. I sincerely believed that I was the better man and that if given the chance, I could take him.

Finally, after many telephone calls, Vince McMahon agreed to arrange a match between me and Buddy Rogers. McMahon realized that I wasn't going to come back to New York for anything less.

THE MATCH OF MY LIFE

After getting McMahon's commitment for the title match, I sat down with Frank Tunney and explained everything to him. I was going to leave the final decision up to him. I owed him all the success that I had known up to that point. He had given me a chance to excel in my profession and nobody had ever done that before. I certainly didn't want to do anything that would hurt Frank in any way.

I told him all that McMahon had said...how Vince wanted me to come back to New York and how he had agreed to put me in the ring with Buddy Rogers for the title. I told Frank that I really believed that I could take that belt and with it, build a career.

Frank looked at me and smiled, "You're right of course. With that championship belt, you'd be a smash draw. I'll agree to release you, but can you do something for me?"

"What's that, Frank?" I wanted to know. "Just come back up here every two weeks and wrestle for my big show. That's all I ask." I shook his hand and gave him my personal guarantee. "This I will do for you, Frank. You can trust me on it." He seemed genuinely happy for me and said, "Your word is good enough for me, Bruno. Good luck in New York." With that, I phoned McMahon the next day and told him that I had made all the proper arrangements with Frank Tunney. In exchange for allowing me to return to the States, I had agreed to travel every second Sunday to the Maple Leaf Gardens in Toronto and wrestle on Frank's main card. McMahon quickly approved these terms. Before I hung up, I asked him again, "Is my match against Rogers guaranteed?" McMahon assured me that it was. Getting Rogers into the ring to wrestle me was harder than McMahon had anticipated. Rogers had as much dislike for me as I did for him. And Buddy was not very anxious to meet me for the title. I'll say this for him...he was a very cagey, ring-wise veteran who always seemed to find a way to save his championship belt. He always knew that if it got too nasty for him in the ring, he could find a way to get a disqualification and wipe out the match. I knew that Rogers saw me as a young and powerful opponent, but he never saw me as someone capable of defeating him. He felt that I lacked the knowledge and skills necessary to take him down.

Somehow or other, McMahon talked Rogers into meeting me. Whether or not he played on the man's vanity or appealed to his pride, I don't know, but he got him to commit. The day of reckoning was set for May 17, 1963 at the site of the old Madison Square Garden on 38th Street, right in the heart of New York. My attitude was simple. If I was going to meet a lion, I would defeat that lion.

In February of '63, I returned from Canada and began to wrestle again in my old territory. I vowed to take the next three months and sharpen my skills, work on my strength and pump myself up mentally for the Rogers match.

It was shortly after I had gotten back that I ran into Buddy Rogers in Pittsburgh at the Civic Arena. I was appearing in a preliminary bout one night and just as I was about to go on, I saw Rogers enter the Arena. He was dressed to the teeth, smoking a big cigar. He stepped out into passageway and surveyed the crowd.

It was almost showtime and the place was practically empty...maybe two thousand fans in an Arena that could hold nearly ten thousand. What happened next fills me with anger whenever I think about it.

Rogers says to himself, "Who wants to wrestle for an empty house?" So he goes and tells the Doctor on duty that he was having some chest pains and he wanted to excuse himself for the night. He thought that the Doctor would say, "Don't wrestle tonight and see how you feel tomorrow."

The Doctor did excuse Rogers that evening, but instead of forgetting about it, he went to Commissioner Solomon in Pittsburgh and told him about Rogers' chest pains. Commissioner Solomon was known as a tough, strict overseer and when he heard this, he suspended Buddy Rogers' license until such time as Rogers could receive a medical examination and a clean bill of health. Solomon contacted all the other Commissioners around the country and within twenty-four hours, Rogers was suspended. He had outfoxed himself.

McMahon was furious. Here was his star attraction, a so-called tough guy whose license had been lifted for medical reasons. McMahon herded Rogers into Georgetown Hospital in Washington, D.C. and ran him through a complete medical examination...which he passed with flying colors.

After that report came back from the hospital, Rogers was reinstated nationwide. He went back to wrestling his regular card, crushing his opponents, looking ahead to his match with me with growing concern.

At last, the night of the match arrived...May 17th, 1963. For a while, waiting in my dressing room, I heard reports that Rogers wasn't going to show up. Since the championship bout was the last match scheduled for the evening, 1 had plenty of time to think about what had happened to me since I had turned pro in November of '59.

I thought about the struggles, the hardships, the suffering...and I thought about my wife and child. My God, I remember thinking, this night is what

62

it's all about. To get to this level still isn't enough. I've got to make it work. If I fail now, there'll be no second chances.

All these ideas were colliding with each other in my head as I waited for my match. Before this night, I was striving to do anything to get to this point and now I was saying to myself, "What if it doesn't work?"

By the time the trainer came and knocked on the dressing room door, I was pumped up higher than I've ever been before. I knew I couldn't lose that night. I'd worked too long and too hard to fall short.

When I got into the ring with Rogers, I couldn't wait for that bell to ring. I came in like a tank! That's the truth...like a tank! I grabbed for Rogers and his reaction confused me. He stood frozen, not moving.

Then I dove straight at him and scooped him up with every bit of strength that I had, throwing him onto my shoulder. I screamed at him over the roar of the crowd, "Give up or I'll break your back!"

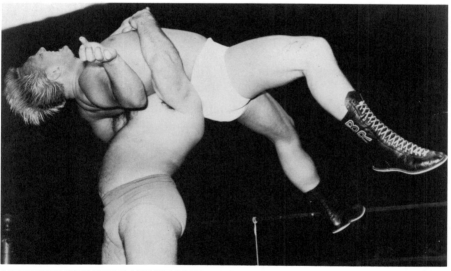

MADISON SQUARE GARDEN MAY 17, 1963
Bruno Sammartino defeated Buddy Rogers for the World Wrestling Championship before a capacity attendance of 19,639

63

A stunned Buddy Rogers remains on the mat as the new champion raises his arms to the fans.

And he submitted. Like a lamb to the slaughter, he gave up. Within 48 seconds, Buddy Rogers was defeated and Bruno Sammartino was the new champion!

I thought the roof was going to pop off the Garden. The crowd noise was incredible. When they put the belt around my waist, it was a great, great feeling. I was thrilled beyond belief because I had always known in my heart that this moment would happen.

For ten or fifteen minutes, I couldn't leave the ring to go back to my dressing room. My compatriots, my Italian fans, rushed in and raised me up on their shoulders, parading me around for the world to see. The police finally had to call for reinforcements to free me.

But while all this was happening, I suddenly got a chill, that same cold feeling that had visited me before as I waited for the match to begin. This was the top, but what if I fall to some other opponent my next time out? What if the fans forget me? What happens if I can't fill the arenas like I did in Canada?

When the police got me back in my dressing room at last, I closed the door behind me and just sank down into a chair. I sat there for a long time, thinking, letting everything soak in.

After a while, everybody in the Garden was gone except me. I got up from my chair and went to take my shower. I muttered to myself, "This is what you wanted! Stop being so negative! Remember what you did in Toronto. If it worked there, it can work in New York."

I reminded myself of the huge Italian population in New York, the support that they would give me. How El Progresso, the Italian newspaper based in New York, would back me. I started getting that adrenalin pumping again, thinking about what lay ahead for me. I pushed the negative thoughts out of my mind.

I got dressed, packed my little duffle bag and walked out of the Garden. Now, the house was empty and most of the lights were off. The only sound was the echo of my footsteps.

I decided to walk back to my room on 42nd Street from where the Garden was on 38th. I was staying at a cheap hotel because I guess I still felt very insecure about my chances before the bout began. The run-down room had matched my mood.

As I headed back, I tried to put everything in perspective. After all the suffering I had put myself and my family through, after those seven months of hell while I lived under the shame of an illegal suspension, after skirting around the country not having money to stay in a decent hotel or even to buy a meal, after all that...was the misery finally coming to an end?

As I passed a phone booth, I suddenly stopped and thought, "Oh, my God, I've got to call my family and tell them what's happened."

I dialed my Mom and Dad's number and let the phone ring for what seemed like a very long time. My wife and I didn't even have a phone at the time and whenever I called, I'd have to phone my parents and then they would run upstairs to our second floor apartment and tell Carol that I was on the line.

My sister, Mary, who lived across the street, answered the phone. At first I thought I might have dialed her number by mistake since the two numbers were similar.

When she answered and heard my voice, she screamed, "Bruno! Oh, my God!" and I thought, "What the heck's wrong with her?"

She stammered, "My God, Bruno. They just said on the Eleven O'clock News that you won the title in Madison Square Garden!"

I couldn't believe it. "They did! They announced it on TV?"

"Yes, Bruno. They said on the news that you beat Buddy Rogers in 48 seconds and now you're the new heavyweight champion of the world! Mom and Pop are here now. Bruno, they're so proud of you!" I said, "So everybody knows already! I didn't think this was going to make the news

65

Being the world's heavyweight champion still hadn't sunk in.

in Pittsburgh.'' My Dad got on the phone next and said, ''Son, we are all very proud of you. We are toasting you with a glass of wine right this minute.'' Then my Mom took the phone and she asked me in a tiny voice, ''Bruno...si fatemale? Did you get hurt or anything?'' I laughed and told her, ''No, Mom...I didn't get hurt.'' 'Nothing hurts?'' she wanted to know. ''No, Mom...nothing hurts. It was a short match...only 48 seconds. He never did a thing to me. I did it all to him.'' And I could hear her saying, ''Oh, thank God! Thank God!'' After I hung up and continued walking back to my hotel, I thought, ''Wow! That's great! They know all about it back in Pittsburgh.''

Right around the corner from my hotel there was a small hole-in-the-wall deli where they sold fried chickens, prepared on a rotary spit. To celebrate, I went in and bought two birds, got a half gallon of orange juice and went up to my room with my feast. I sat there on the edge of the bed, ate my chickens, drank my orange juice and watched the postage stamp size television on the dresser. After I finished my victory meal, I felt very tired and I went right to sleep.

I got up pretty early the next morning. Champion or not, I had a match scheduled that evening at the Sunnyside Gardens and the bout was to be telecast. I went over to the gym that I frequented in New York called the Mid City Health Club. I wanted to pump a little iron to keep myself fine-tuned.

I guess winning the championship still hadn't sunk in. As I walked over to the Club, I remember wondering if anybody else besides my family in Pittsburgh and the fans at the Garden last night knew about my victory.

My question was answered as soon as I walked into the gym. All of the guys started screaming, "Congratulations!" I was just amazed. Everybody kept coming over and pounding me on the back. It took quite a while to get through my routine that morning.

After I left the gym, I took a short cut back to the hotel. On my way back later that morning, now people were yelling at me, "Hey, Bruno! Congratulations, Bruno!" When I sat down to eat at a restaurant, all of a sudden I was getting recognition from everywhere. I just kept thinking to myself, "Wow!"

As I came out for my match that evening at Sunnyside Gardens, the crowd stood up and began chanting my name, "Bruno! Bruno! Bruno!" I never had expected this kind of impact from winning the championship belt. Never! It had happened so quickly!

Lady Luck started to run with me. Before my victory over Buddy Rogers, Capitol had been near bankruptcy. Their business had been sinking lower and lower into the ground.

Now, thanks to the generous support of many fans, particularly the Italians, the wrestling turnstiles began to spin faster and faster. These were the fans who believed in me and what I was accomplishing. And they remembered me from before my suspension...a struggling young Italian kid who had hooked up with the giant, Haystacks Calhoun one night...and lifted him off the mat.

The fans never forgot that. Even when I defeated Buddy Rogers, they still remembered me as the guy who picked up Haystacks Calhoun...and as the guy who did push-ups with two men sitting on his back.

Maybe I should say a word here about Haystacks. Calhoun weighed over 625 pounds and the feeling was that nobody but nobody could take him up into the air. Not even Olympic weightlifter Paul Anderson could do that when he was wrestling.

I certainly don't think that it's fair to say that Anderson lacked the strength to lift Calhoun. The problem was just the simple mechanics of leverage. Anderson was only five feet nine inches or so, weighing close to 370 pounds himself. With Calhoun tipping the scales at 625 pounds, there was just no way that two wrestlers of that enormous size were going to be able to reach around each other, hold on and lift.

On the other hand, I was taller and lighter than Haystacks and surely just as powerful, if not more so. At six feet tall, I weighed 270 pounds and because I didn't have his bulkiness, I was able to outmaneuver Calhoun.

Haystacks Calhoun

The night of our match, just when Haystacks thought he had my number, getting me in a side headlock, I was able to bearhug Haystacks' thigh and with that leverage, I scooped him up into the air. When I did that, Madison Square Garden nearly came tumbling down from the crowd noise.

So after I won the title and started to defend it, much to my surprise the fans started pouring in to see me. In the first few months after the Rogers match, I tested myself on a few minor contenders and won handily. The first big defense occurred about four months into my reign in September, 1963.

I took on Killer Kowalski at Madison Square Garden in the first of what was to be many, many matches with this man. Killer was a very unusual wrestler, actually a vegetarian although I have no idea if that's what contributed to his magnificent conditioning. He stood about six feet seven inches tall, weighed around 280 pounds and was known as a machine in the ring.

68

Killer Kowalski and I do battle outside the ring.

Killer did no physical training or road work and he was not a weightlifter either. From what I understand, he practiced aerobic training...a discipline that wasn't popular at the time but is big today. He would do his sit-ups, his push-ups, all his training in private.

I knew that he had extremely strong hands, too. I heard that he used to take newspapers, starting with the first page and with his hands, just keep crunching and crunching until he would have the whole paper in a ball. And he was always squeezing tennis balls which gave him a tremendous grip. Thanks to this specialized training, Killer developed a hold he called the claw that was devastating if you got caught in it.

Killer got his nickname because of a match he had against another very powerful man, Eric Holmback, who was known in wrestling circles as Yukon Eric. Yukon Eric weighed around 300 pounds, but was only about six feet three inches tall. Eric looked like a lumberjack with those lumberjack shirts with the sleeves torn off. He always wore jeans and boots and for him, that was no gimmick. That was Yukon Eric.

I remember meeting Yukon Eric in Ontario. After he finished wrestling, he would rush out into the freezing night air, jump naked into a nearby lake, swim across the lake and back, then climb back into his jeans and shirt and go about his business. He was a real outdoorsman.

Eric also owned some very bad cauliflowered ears, churned into that condition from years of wrestling. Killer Kowalski, in a match with Yukon Eric, actually ripped off Eric's right ear. Pulled it clean away. After that Kowalski was known as the Killer. In later years, if you ever saw Yukon Eric, you would have noticed that his dark blonde hair was longer on the right side of his face. He grew his hair that way to cover up his missing ear.

So here it was September of '63...four months into my championship reign and my Madison Square Garden match with Kowalski was a sellout. At that time, Killer was one of wrestling's biggest draws. Yet even though my name was relatively brand-new to many people, the fans were really rallying to my support. This particular bout which pitted young champ against established star seemed to catch the public's attention.

Our battle was a continuous blur of action. Kowalski's reputation as a human dynamo was well deserved. I remember many of the other wrestlers watching us that night from the wings, wondering which wrestler was going to run out of steam first.

The fans erupted into cheers everytime I laid a finger on Killer. I think the crowd really wanted to see me defend my title with a vengeance. Finally, after close to 40 minutes of non-stop wrestling, I pinned Kowalski for a count of three and walked away to the roar of the crowd.

After I established myself as a serious champion, someone who was going to defend his belt ferociously, the fans filled the arenas to see me perform. That's when I told Vince McMahon that I wanted to cut down on the number of television appearances I was making.

I didn't think it was wise to have so much exposure on television. I was wrestling no-name guys week in and week out and I was showing up on the tube almost every weekend.

If the people wanted to see me wrestle, let then come to the arenas. That was the name of the game. Fill the arenas and let television serve as the promotional tool. And McMahon agreed. How could he argue with success?

So in 1963 and 1964, the same years that the Beatles got hot, my career caught fire. I started selling out Philadelphia's Convention Center and Pittsburgh's Civic Arena and Baltimore's Civic Center or wherever I was going. It was fantastic!

Then I went to Japan and did phenomenal business there. In Australia, arenas were sold out every night for the entire month I was there. I then went to South America and was also well received.

I was wrestling every single night for months at a time , sometimes twice a day. It was absolutely one of the best periods in my life. Success became one of my favorite words.

GOING BACK HOME

The appearance schedule that I took on after I won the championship was starting to take its toll. Month in and month out, I wrestled almost daily. I was upset that I wasn't able to see my wife Carol and my son David very much and I began to think about taking a break from it all. The chance to do that came from an unlikely fan.

I'm talking about Monsignor Fusco from the Pittsburgh diocese. He would come to the Civic Arena to see me wrestle and eventually we met and became good friends.

The first time we had lunch together, Monsignor Fusco blew my mind. First, he said he had met Primo Carnera many years ago. And if that wasn't enough, he said that he understood that I was an opera lover, which I was. He went on to say that he had personally known the world-famous Italian tenor, Enrico Caruso. To think that he had acutally spoken to those two giants in their professions. Well, we had lunch together many times and I was always fascinated with the stories he would tell.

Monsignor Fusco was just one of the nicest men you could ever meet. He mentioned how he had gone back to Italy many times and I certainly envied him for that. Little did I realize how powerful a man he was in the Catholic Church and that many of those trips were on Church business to the Vatican.

One time he said to me and this was in the early part of 1966, "Bruno, my boy." That was his favorite expression. "Have you ever gone back to Italy since you came over as a boy?"

I replied sadly, "No, Monsignor. I've not gone back."

"Well, are you planning on going back?" he asked.

I shrugged. "Yes, eventually. I very much would like to go back and see my family...but right now, it's so hectic. My schedule is so crazy."

Monsignor Fusco smiled broadly. "Well, Bruno...when you do, please let me know about your plans...because I would like to arrange for you to meet the Pope!

I stared at him in disbelief. I thought to myself, "Come on." I know he's an influencial man, but LIKE THAT?" I said, "Monsignor, are you telling me that if I went back to the Old Country that I could have a private audience with the Pope?"

"Absolutely" he said. "I can arrange it."

I blurted, "Monsignor, if you can arrange this, it would be the highest honor that I've ever known."

"No trouble, Bruno, my boy," said Monsignor Fusco. "Just find out when you can travel, and I'll take care of the rest."

The very first chance I could, I sat down with Vince McMahon in his office in Washington, D.C. I told him that my schedule was getting too ridiculous and that I wanted to take a break...just for one week...and fly back to Italy. I told him that this was the chance of a lifetime because I had somebody working for me to arrange to see the Pope. Besides that, it would give me the opportunity to return to my hometown and visit with my friends and relatives whom I hadn't seen since I was fourteen years old.

Vince thought it over for a few seconds and said, "Okay, we'll work it out for you." He didn't go into specifics at the time, but later I found out that he had definite ulterior motives.

At any rate, McMahon and I figured out the timing and once that was settled, I got in touch with the Monsignor. He told me that he had a good friend in Rome, who would drive me wherever I wanted to go and he mentioned that he'd arrange for a suite for me and my family at the Excelsior Hotel in Veno Viento. All I could say was, "Great! That's great!"

After alerting my family in Pizzoferrato that I was coming back for a visit, my wife and I packed our bags and made all the necessary preparations to get ready for the trip. Even though our son David was only five and a half years old, we weren't going to let him miss out on the adventure.

We flew to Rome on March 25th, 1966 and went straight to our Hotel to unwind. After a good night's sleep, the very next day I had a call from a Vatican spokesman, acknowledging that Monsignor Fusco had been in touch with them. He went on to say that our Papal audience would be in three days and that they would get back to me for the final arrangements. After I hung up, I was elated. It really was going to happen...an audience with the Pope.

Then an hour or so later, the phone rang again. He said his name was John and that he was a friend of Monsignor Fusco. He turned out to be the man whom Monsignor Fusco had contacted to drive us around. Actually that was his business. John had a fleet of cars and he would take tourists all over the countryside for a fee of $25 a day...and you would have him at your beck and call for up to ten hours a day. Today, for similar service in Italy, you'd have to cough up $200 to $300 per day. Quite a difference.

The next morning John picked us up and began showing us all of the sights. He took us to some great restaurants for both lunch and dinner. We kicked around Rome for two whole days and the experience was just wonderful.

Then the hallowed day arrived. John drove us to the Vatican itself. I remember we waited in a small room with Monsignor Rocco and my wife and I were getting more nervous by the minute. Finally, the time came and we were called in to see His Holiness, Pope Paul the Sixth. Monsignor Rocco escorted us into an adjoining room where we waited for his entrance.

Both me and my wife had considered beforehand what we would say and do when we went in, but we were terribly nervous about it. I remember saying to John in the car on the way over, "I'm very nervous. What's appropriate and what's not appropriate to do when you meet the Pope?"

John laughed and said, "Just relax. When you go in, the first thing you do is bow. Then you kiss his ring and greet him." Then John added, "Don't be afraid because he will talk to you. He will ask questions. He will talk.

With John's advice in mind, I began rehearsing what I was going to say to the Pope. I thought I'd say, after I kissed his ring, "Holy Father, this is the experience of my life. Never did I ever think that I was going to have such a great honor. I was born here in Italy and then I went to America as a young boy and who would have ever thought that such a boy could grow up and meet with you, Holy Father."

Yes, that sounded good to me. I would give that speech exactly. Well, what happened didn't exactly go according to plan.

My wife, Carol, was sitting there with our son, David, in the meeting room

David at a very young age strikes a wrestling pose.

73

and I stood right behind their chair. When Pope Paul entered, we did as we had been told by our driver, John. I kissed his ring after Carol did and then the strangest thing happened. My wife and I were both nearly paralyzed. We couldn't say anything.

David five and a half years old then, just looked at Pope Paul and said, "Hey, I remember you. I saw you on television!"

The Pope had made a visit to the United States about six months prior to our trip to Italy. Of course, the television coverage had been enormous.

I thought to myself, "Oh, boy, David. Nice move!"

But the Pope laughed and then asked in Italian what our son's name was.

With a quavering voice, I answered, "Davida," then I added, "My wife's name is Carolina and I am Bruno Sammartino." At that point I managed to say what a great honor it was to meet him.

Carol never spoke a word. She was absolutely frozen. I began to tell him about the profession I was in and I got the feeling, though I'm not positive, that the Pope was not overly thrilled about me choosing such a violent way to earn a living. As we talked, David kept interrupting, asking, "What's this?" and "What's that?" The Pope seemed to be such a saintly person and he took very kindly to our son. Once he asked David a question about his school. Just before we concluded our audience, we had our picture taken with Pope Paul. I had arranged for this to happen before our meeting. I had been told that they were not willing to allow photographs to be taken if the pictures were going to be used in any way for publicity or to advance my career.

I assured the Pope's people that I would never use them while I was a professional wrestler for any publicity in any way, shape or form. I said that these pictures would be something that I and my family will cherish for the rest of our lives. With my guarantee not to benefit from their public use, permission was given and the photographs were taken.

Our audience lasted perhaps only ten or fifteen minutes. When it did end, Carol kissed his ring. She had kissed his ring when we entered and kissed his ring when we left and never opened her mouth in between...not one time.

When we walked out of the room, Carol and I were both trembling. It was a feeling that's very difficult to describe...kind of thrilled with what had happened yet disappointed in some ways. There was so much we had wanted to say and didn't.

The next day John picked us up at our hotel and we were off to visit Pizzoferrato...my old home town. We had been joined by my Uncle who had traveled into Rome from Pizzoferrato to greet us.

On the way, we stopped in Casino which was a village I remembered well.

During the war, it had been one of the most bombarded areas in all of Italy. During the battle for Monte Casino, thousands of men on both sides were killed.

When my Mother, sister Mary, brother Paul and I, had passed through the village on our way to America, it was nothing but rubble. All we saw were stones, tossed by the bombs into an awful sculpture of destruction. In fact, the battle that had raged there left nothing standing.

On our journey back though in 1966, Casino had become a beautiful city again. I was so impressed by the effort that it must have taken to resurrect the town.

We stopped in Casino for lunch and while we were eating, I noticed that after my Uncle had excused himself from our table, he had made a beeline for a telephone. In fact, he had been on the phone several other times that morning. I didn't know what he was up to. Being polite, of course I didn't ask him.

After lunch, we climbed back in the car and began driving again. Finally, I spotted La Torra, the mountain in which our town was cradled. La Torra went straight up into the air. You had to climb it from the back because from the front, the mountain was one long plunge.

At one point, we passed the site where my father had been born. His little home was still there and the tiny church that my Uncle, the priest, Don Vincenzo Sammartino, had built with his own hands. It was also at this place during the war where a furious battle had been fought. We had found many, many bodies inside and outside the church.

We passed the church and pressed on. Up and up into the mountains we drove. Then at last we pulled in the town square, La Piazza. That's where I found out the reason that my Uncle had been making all those phone calls. He was arranging my homecoming.

Waiting for us in the square were all of the townspeople. Everyone had taken the day off from work and they were all assembled in front of the town's new Municipal Building. Talk about getting goose bumps! I was overwhelmed by it all...speechless almost like I was with the Pope.

I stepped out of the car and started to recognize people that I remembered from so many years ago. Then out of the crowd came an old man that I didn't recognize immediately. He was thin, weighing no more than 110 pounds and his walk was unsteady.

He called out my name and then I realized that this was my precious Uncle Camillo. He had always been like a father to me. Certainly he was the kindest human being that I've ever met in my life. We embraced and as I hugged him, we both began to cry.

Our home in Pizzoferrato as it looked during my return trip to the Old Country.

I found out later that the reason he had shriveled down to almost nothing from the robust, handsome man he'd been, was that he was a dying man. He had stomach cancer and the illness had nearly taken its toll completely. The man that I had loved so dearly had been brought low by this killing disease.

And then I saw my mother's sister, Aunt Agnes there, too. And we all cried some more.

We went into the Municipal Building because the town officials wanted to formally greet me there. Speeches were made saying how proud everyone was of Bruno Sammartino's accomplishments as a champion...and how much honor I had brought to them.

Everything was completely unexpected. I probably came across that first day as a big idiot because I was absolutely speechless. I was so overpowered that I just stood in my place and kept saying hello to all the people.

We stayed for several days and as our stay lengthened, I began to meet everyone more informally. I wanted to share memories with my old friends and relatives and I wanted to meet all the rest...their children and grand-children. I definitely didn't want to leave my home town behind with the impression that here I was some kind of big shot. Everyone told me though that I was still the same kid that they remembered.

I went to all their homes to have a little coffee with everyone and talk. Of course, all of my relatives were fighting over who would have us for lunch and who would have us for dinner.

One memory that I had from when I was a little boy was how excited we were about anyone who had just come back from America. Whoever this person was, we imagined we knew him just by the way he walked...a special walk that spoke of worldly wisdom and we liked to follow him around town, probably hoping that some of the magic would rub off on us.

Often, I recall, the people whom we tagged along behind would throw us pennies so we could buy candy. There was a favorite local store in town where basic foods were sold and where a jar of penny candy lay hidden under the counter. We would dash to the store to spend these special bits of cash.

All these memories came flooding back because as soon as I would leave the little hotel where we were staying, little kids would be waiting for me on the street outside my door. The first day I gave five or six of them each a dollar from America. In 1966, a dollar was worth about 500 lira and 500 lira was fantastic to them. These kids looked at the money and felt like, my God, they were rich now.

The next day fifteen kids showed up at the hotel to greet me so I gave each of them a dollar. I guess I started looking like the Pied Piper with all these children trailing behind me. My wife Carol was amazed by it all. I told her that by watching those kids she was watching me as a kid, too.

When we left after spending nearly four days there, it was a very tough feeling to handle. Again, the whole town had taken off from work and they all assembled once more in the town square to say goodbye.

It was so very painful too because I knew I'd never see my Uncle Camillo again. Most fathers were not as good as he was. I hugged him close to say goodbye. He was so choked up he couldn't speak, couldn't say goodbye. He just stood there, not moving.

We finished saying goodbye and giving our thanks to all the townspeople for being so gracious during our stay there. As our car pulled away, I looked back to see my Uncle Camillo, his eyes following us as we rounded the corner and headed back to Rome.

That was the last time I saw him. As I grew up, he had given me love and understanding. Uncle Camillo was just simply a special human being. I still miss him very much.

Rome always fascinated me. As a child, I loved to read about ancient history. During our visit, I had hoped to spend more time in the city, visiting the Colosseum, the Catacombs or Caesar's Forum. But because I had not been aware of how ill my Uncle was, the last couple of days in Italy were very dreary for me.

Finally, after a week that I'll never forget, my family and I returned to America. The very next day, I left on tour for Australia.

Before I left though, I checked in with Vince McMahon on the phone He asked me how the trip went.

"Fantastic," I said.

Before I could go into detail, he butted in. "Did you get pictures of you and the Pope?" he wanted to know.

"Yes, they gave us permission to take some."

"Great," he said, "Now here's what I want you to do. Get a few dozen copies made and then mail them to. ..."

"Wait a second, Vince. Hold on! I'm not mailing those photos anywhere." I'm not back one hour and already McMahon's getting me steamed up.

"What do you mean, Bruno? Those pictures would be incredible publicity."

I just said no to him. "I gave my word that those pictures would never be used for promotion as long as I was a professional wrestler. I promised the Pope that I would not do that. Just forget it, Vince."

I hung up the phone, packed my suitcases for Australia and tried not to let McMahon get to me. After I returned from my trip, the pictures of our audience with the Pope were waiting for me. They were beautiful and clearly showed me, Carol and David with Pope Paul. I went out and had some 8X10s made but under no circumstances was I going to give them to the media.

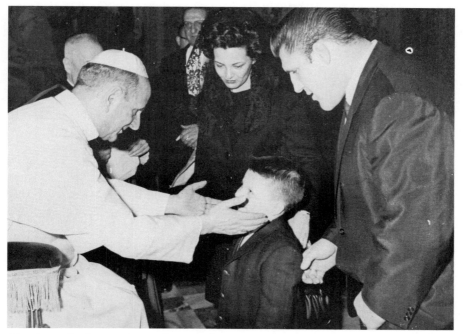

Now it can be shown. A rare photograph of our audience with Pope Paul VI.

Then I found out that my Papal audience had been publicized anyway while I was gone. Some newspaper man had asked me questions about it. I called up McMahon and asked him, "What's going on, Vince?"

McMahon answered, quick as you please, "Well, Bruno, you said you weren't allowed to use the pictures, but I'm sure the Pope didn't mean that you had to keep the whole meeting secret."

I could sense that Vince wasn't being sarcastic when he said that. I answered, "Well, you've got me there. Nobody said anything about that...but just realize, I am not going to have those pictures used for any reason." Vince surprised me.

He paused, then said, "Well, if you made that promise and you feel that strongly, then I guess there's nothing I can do about it."

79

So we never did use them. And you know what, holding to my promise caused me grief with the media. Newspaper reporters would come up to me and say sarcastically, "Hey, Bruno, I understand I you had an audience with the Pope when you were in Italy recently. And that you had pictures taken. How about letting us take a look at them?" I told them of my promise. I was even afraid to just let them look at them for fear somehow a copy would be made. So these guys went away and wrote negative things about me, saying that I had claimed to meet with the Pope and that I claimed to have pictures and that I claimed to have made a promise not to show the pictures. Most of this nonsensical criticism came from New York writers. But even the writers in Pittsburgh, my home town, leveled the same charges. I just had to take it because well, how can you break your promise to the Pope?

REMEMBERING THE GREAT ONES

As a child in Italy, my idol was Primo Carnera. The people would tell fantastic stories about this hulk of a man and I would listen to them all with the wide eyes of a young boy. If they would have told me that he was twenty feet tall, I would have believed it.

In reality, Carnera was about six feet seven inches and weighed 270 pounds at the most. In today's wrestling world, Primo would be no giant. What made him stand out was his lean, big-boned physique...and for somebody from Italy, there's never been anybody bigger. I always dreamed that I would be like him some day.

As I grew into my profession as a wrestler, besides Primo Carnera there were a number of other competitors in the business who made their impact on me. When I was first coming up, Gorgeous George and Antonio Rocca seemed to me to represent the best in my sport.

An incident happened soon after I had turned pro that gave me a very different slant on the realities of wrestling. It occurred in December of 1959 after I had been in the professional ring no more than a month and a half.

McMahon had booked me into the Convention Center in Philadelphia against Gorgeous George. I was elated because here I was still wet behind the ears and now I was slated to take on someone of the stature of this man.

Well, what didn't immediately sink in for me was that Gorgeous George was no longer in his prime even though I was aware that he was nearly 42 years old in late '59. I do remember thinking that 42 seemed pretty old for a pro wrestler. I guess to a young kid like me anything over 25 seemed ancient.

The bout turned out to be a painful experience. When I wrestled him, I was surprised to find out that the legendary Gorgeous George weighed no more than 215 pounds and was only five feet ten inches tall, if that.

He was a very capable wrestler though, but a lot of his fair-weather fans didn't seem to think so anymore. Other fans were even more critical. All they saw when they looked at Gorgeous George was a gimmick...a guy dressed in fancy robes who strutted around the ring, smelling perfume and tossing back his curly blonde hair.

His real name was George Wagner and early in his wrestling career, he found himself getting nowhere even though he had great skills. Then a friend of George's, a chef in a restaurant where he ate, said to him, "You know, George, if you did something that would bring attention to yourself, it might just help you become a hit."

George asked his friend if he had any suggestions and the chef said "I've got just the thing for you. You have a great head of hair. Why don't you let it grow longer, curl it, bleach it, then you put on this big, fancy robe...."

As they say, the rest is history. George followed the chef's advice to the letter and he became a big drawing card for years. As time wore on, some fans began to get on his case for his so-called arrogance yet most seemed to still respect his wrestling abilities.

As time marched on and other stars took the spotlight, George started to fade away into the shadows. So when I met him at the Philadelphia Convention Center, he was no longer on top. Far from it. I hadn't realized that he no longer had the big name across the country.

To me, young Bruno Sammartino, who had read and heard about the man, meeting Gorgeous George in the ring was a thrill. The painful thing was that when I was actually wrestling this legend, shooting back and forth on the canvas, I could hear catcalls coming out of the dark, yelling for me to be careful or I'd hurt the old man. And some fans hollered for me to "take care of that little dried-out...so-and-so."

Really nasty names that I don't care to repeat. It got to me and I remember thinking, "My God, is this what happens to you at the other end of the tunnel?"

I beat him that night. I took him up in the air for a backbreaker. Yes, I won but it wasn't a wonderful feeling at all. I honestly felt lousy about it.

After the match, I went back to my dressing room, knowing that George must have heard those remarks as well as I did. I wondered what it had done to him? I never found out because when I came out of my dressing room, he had already left the building.

A few months later, in 1960, I not only got the chance to meet my boyhood idol but actually became his tag team partner for a while. Of course, I'm talking about Primo Carnera.

McMahon dreamed up the team. Because Primo was still a big name, McMahon wanted to keep him in the ring. Everybody knew that Primo's appeal, especially with the Italians, hadn't diminished even though his abilities had deteriorated to almost nothing.

So they put me, a young Italian guy just coming up, with Carnera in tag team matches. McMahon figured that Carnera would draw the crowds and Sammartino would do the wrestling.

That was the way it was. Carnera was the show case. He would make his entrance into the ring for ten seconds or so, tag out and let Bruno do the wrestling. That was fine with me. l didn't even care if I had to wrestle the whole match by myself. To me it was just such an honor to be on the same team as Primo Carnera. I was so thrilled that even though I knew he was

Primo and Bruno team up. It was a chance to wrestle with my idol.

getting most of the money, it didn't bother me one bit. Even though my own personal situation was bad, I said, "Let Primo get the money. God bless him." He was my hero so all that didn't matter.

I'm sure I would have continued on the Carnera/Sammartino team longer, but again the remarks I heard brought me down. Fans would say, "Primo...Primo. You're too old to wrestle. Why don't you retire instead of hiring this young guy to wrestle for you?"

Hearing those insults aimed at Primo was like putting a knife through my own heart. It bothered me most of all that Primo would hear the same words.

Working with Carnera was a thrill of a lifetime.

My experiences with Gorgeous George and with Primo Carnera reinforced one important principle in me though. I vowed to myself that I would never let happen to me what I had seen happen to those two wrestling greats. I made a solemn promise to get out of wrestling while I was still at the top of my game.

Another legendary character that I met in my rookie year was Antonio Rocca. Rocca was born in Italy, but his family left there when he was sixteen and moved to Buenos Aries, Argentina. There he worked as a tailor in a shop with his father.

Rocca was an excellent athlete, playing soccer and wrestling professionally in Argentina. He came to the United States as a wrestler in 1947 and became an immediate sensation.

His manager was Kola Kwariani, the man who had discovered him in South America, As I'd mentioned earlier, I was to have my own personal dealings with Kwariani, but that was later down the road.

Kwariani was this burley Russian who had also immigrated to America to cash in on his own wrestling prowess. He actually had been touring Argentina when, by chance, he caught Rocca on the same card as he was appearing.

A few years later when Kwariani was getting too old to wrestle, Kola decided to pursue promotion and managing and he remembered Rocca as somebody with extra special talents. Kola worked things out and brought Rocca to the states where he began to personally manage Rocca's career.

I was quite excited about meeting Rocca when the chance came. I idolized him much like I did Primo Carnera, but for an Italian, he was a bit of a typical Latino.

A chance to team up with another wrestling great . . . Antonio Rocca.

I was even his tag team partner a few times. I'll say this...Rocca was always in great condition and always gave his matches all that he had. It was his wrestling skills that I questioned, frankly. By no means was he a poor wrestler. I mean to say he was more of an acrobat...an aerialist. In this, he could pull off phenomenal stunts that nobody else could.

The only negative that I will say about Rocca was that I sensed as the years went on, he was the kind of guy who didn't like to share the spotlight with anybody. He certainly didn't want to see a young wrestler like me become a threat to his throne. When I found this out later his attitude disappointed me.

Rocca went on to have a great career...until he aged to the point where he couldn't do those incredible aerialistic feats that he once was able to do. Because of that, he was forced to retire.

Sadly, I later found out that the deal he had with his promoters was not a very good one. They actually took two/thirds of his income so that when he retired, his financial condition was poor indeed. That shocked me because I thought wrestling would have made him a wealthy man. After all the name Antonio Rocca had been a top draw for a long time.

The saddest part of the story came a few years after his retirement when he tragically died at the age of forty-seven. The cause was listed as uremic poisoning.

As I think about these greats from my early career, I recall courageous men who have given their all to a profession they loved. In some cases, they continued to wrestle long past their prime because I suppose they couldn't imagine a life without the sport. Mostly, I remember them for their dedication to the fans and to the business of professional wrestling.

That said, now there's something that I better get off my chest...something that has always bothered me.

It's the media journalists...the newspaper reporters, the magazine writers, the television commentators. So often these media experts have said that when professional wrestlers bleed, it wasn't real blood. It was chicken blood or ketchup or blood capsules.

Believe me, I bled. And Gorgeous George and Primo Carnera and Antonio Rocca bled.

Yes, I bled many times and I always say to these so-called experts, if you want to see how I bled, I have a nose that has been busted eleven times. I bled from that nose many, many times whether it came from being broken or just from a good clean shot. It was my blood that flowed.

When I bled from my mouth, it was my blood. And I have scars on my body to show where other blood came from. The blood was real.

Now if such a thing as a blood capsule was ever used in the ring, I don't know. I sure can't speak for the whole history of professional wrestling. I myself have never, never seen a blood capsule in my life. Whether anybody wants to believe me or not, that's up to them. I'm telling the absolute truth...I've never seen them used!

Another phony issue that the media have drummed up is whether or not wrestlers have used razor blades to open cuts during a match and bloody themselves up. Again if such a thing has happened, I don't know about it.

Once I asked a reporter who claimed that razor blades were used in the ring, "Okay, where do they get the blade to cut themselves?"

He replied, "That's easy. They tape the blade to their wrist or next to their finger."

I find it bizarre to suggest that somebody can conceal a blade on some part of his body, then while furious action is going on, unravel the tape, start cutting himself and not be seen. It's ridiculous!

Right now, I'd like anybody that can do so, come forward and tell me that they honestly ever saw me go into a match with a taped finger or tape on my wrist.

Of course, nobody can because it never happened. My point is that if razor blades are used by some wrestlers, then I am unaware of it. Since I've not been involved in every match that ever took place around the world, I can't take an oath and say that blades or capsules have never been used. What I'm saying is that I've never seen it.

Another criticism of professional wrestling that I've heard leveled is this. The way wrestling works is that a wrestler wins here in Pittsburgh one night and then loses tomorrow in New York City. That's the way the game goes, the critics say.

Of course, to anybody who has ever said that I say, "Sheer nonsense!" If anybody looks at the records of wrestlers like Antonio Rocca, Lou Thez, Verne Gagna, Don Leo Jonathan, Big Bill Miller or Gorilla Monsoon, you'll see a win/loss ratio that's fantastic. In these athletes' careers, you'll see that they lost very few matches.

I would point to my own professional record, too. As far as pins or submissions, I never submitted once in my life. If I've ever been pinned, it was only three or four times in all over my entire 23-year long career.

What does this all mean then? I feel that any guy in my era who made it to the top got there because he was the better athlete than all the rest. I'm not suggesting that promoters have never asked wrestlers to lose matches. But I was never involved in any bout where the promoter told this wrestler that he had to lose tonight or where he paid that wrestler so much money to take a fall.

I'm not saying that this kind of thing didn't go on. I can only speak from my own personal experience. 1 was never asked to lose by any promoter. Even if a promoter would have asked me to lose, the only way that would have happened would have been if my opponent had been a better wrestler than I was on that particular night.

And if anybody was paid to lose to me, then the promoter was an idiot for throwing away his money. In my prime, I believe I could have beaten anybody anyway. So nobody would have had to be paid off to lose to me.

Of course, I can only speak to my own situation. I do know that other wrestlers have told me that these same kinds of half-truths and outright lies have concerned them also.

All right. Enough of all that.

After I won the Championship in May of '63, I began the long battle to hang on to the belt. Of course, when you're on top, you're the target for everyone else. It was me that everybody wanted to knock off the mountain.

During my first reign as Champion, I wrestled a lot of class individuals. They were all uniquely talented, each one presenting a different challenge to me.

One of those guys who really comes to mind was Big Bill Miller. Big Bill started wrestling professionally while he was still in college. Even as an amateur, he had made his mark early, becoming a Big-10 Champion and a National AU Champion.

Miller was an outstanding athlete as a wrestler and as a football player. He stood about 6 feet 7 inches and weighed around 320 pounds. Just awesome in size, yet his agility startled you.

A couple of years into my first title, Miller finally appeared in the Pittsburgh area and I was slated to wrestle him. I knew that this match was going to be tough if what I had heard about his personality was any indication of the kind of wrestler he was.

I had heard a lot of stuff about him...about his moods and how he was very temperamental, in fact that he had an extremely bad temper. Big Bill had come into professional wrestling with an outstanding amateur background and was starting to be considered one of the best in our business.

Before I met Miller, I had often wondered how to handle somebody like him who not only has the amateur and professional skills that he has, but who is also so large a man. Six feet seven inches tall and 320 pounds is no midget.

His temper also concerned me. I had been told that when Miller got upset, he would lose some of his techniques, but that from all the adrenalin pumping, he would become even stronger and more vicious than ever. In

Big Bill Miller was a tough competitor.

Miller remains on the mat after one of our bouts.

fact, he had a reputation for hurting people.

As I looked at big Bill from across the ring just as our first match was about to begin, I could see you just had to respect him physically. I can imagine why a lot of guys had told me that they were scared stiff once they stepped into the ring with him. He just looked like a guy who came to hurt you and who would enjoy doing it.

What impressed me was his strength. I remember that he picked me up for a body slam. I was around 275 pounds then, but I felt like I was a feather the way he shot me up in the air with such ease. When he slammed me, I felt as though he had thrown me clear across the ring. Awesome!

I noticed that when I out-maneuvered him once or twice, he acted almost as if he were offended by it...and offended in a way that he would really charge into me with a vengence. Once that night he gave me such a kick in my side that I really thought he'd cracked every rib in my chest.

Then because I had this burning sensation in my stomach for days and days, I started to think even more that Big Bill had punctured something in my guts. I went and had X-rays taken but it turned out to be just a bad bruise.

90

Don't get me wrong...I wasn't fearful of Big Bill. I really wasn't. I was never too frightened of any wrestler, but I had greater respect for Miller than most of the other pros from my era.

In my first reign, I wrestled Miller at least two dozen times. I can't remember any match with him where I could say I had it easy. He always gave me a tough night, then the next morning you were sore and ached all over. You knew you'd gone through a war.

Big Bill later left wrestling and today runs a Veterinarian Hospital in Columbus, Ohio.

Another exceptional wrestling talent was Gorilla Monsoon. He was huge, not quite six feet seven inches but weighing over 400 hundred pounds. His detractors said he was just a big, fat slob. Granted, he wasn't a weightlifter, but in his amateur days, he worked out a lot on the mat and he'd developed great stamina for someone of his enormous size.

Gorilla Monsoon

The amazing thing about Gorilla was his agility, a talent that took you by surprise, especially since he had legs like tree trunks, colossal arms, a

91

huge neck and chest. When Gorilla would appear, he'd always want to show the crowd right away just how good an athlete there was inside his immense body. To show off, he'd do cartwheels like a lightweight!

Just to highlight the character of the man for you, one particular time I wrestled him in Madison Square Garden. I thought that if I could explode out of my corner and catch him with a tremendous blow of some kind, then that would really give me the edge in our match. When the bell rang, I shot toward him like a bullet, leaped into the air and caught him with a powerful drop kick.

Evidently, my feet were spread apart more than usual and one foot caught him in the side of the head, while the other smashed him in the upper ribs. He had thrown up an arm to partially block the blow to the head but the kick into his ribs was clean.

I didn't know it until later, but I had cracked two of Gorilla's ribs. The amazing thing was that this was a match to curfew...which in New York City was till 11:00 p.m....and Gorilla kept right on wrestling!

I had always respected Gorilla enormously, but after that night, my admiration for his courage soared. That match lasted for 95 minutes. For over an hour and a half, that man wrestled me tooth and nail and he had two cracked ribs. I've experienced cracked ribs myself and if you want to talk about pain, wow!

There was also considerable danger involved. Gorilla could have punctured a lung, but he never gave up. Even though I thought he was more on the defensive that night than usual, it never occurred to me how much pain he must have been suffering.

Let me take a moment here to say that I myself have never wrestled with the intention of hurting someone on purpose. I always went in to outperform the other guy...to lock him up and pin him, applying sufficient pressure to win a submission. I never ever bore down on anyone, hoping to make something snap. Never.

Not that I haven't hurt people. Not intentionally. But injuries in wrestling are simply a fact of life. It's just the way things happen sometimes.

All in all, Gorilla Monsoon was looked upon as one of the best professional wrestlers of his time because of his awesome size and his great agility. He knew how to use his skills and his enormous bulk so well that he easily could overtake and wear down most opponents who dared enter the ring with him.

Baron Scicluna was another wrestler with outstanding moves. He looked lean at 280 pounds on a six foot five inch frame, but he was very powerful.

I always respected the Baron for his terrific speed. To give you an idea, when I executed an arm drag, I'd pull my opponent right across the ring. Then as I was crossing, I'd spin up on my feet and be right there in a position of advantage. But the Baron was one guy who if I'd catch in an arm drag and then move into my spin, why he'd be right there with me in the proper wrestling position to counter. That's how fast he was.

Occasionally when he began to find himself at a disadvantage in a match, the Baron would become a brawler. He'd switch from beautiful classic wrestling to ugly street brawling in a second.

I wrestled the Baron quite a few times and he gave me lots of problems in those matches. I suppose I showed some "Gorilla Monsoon courage" of my own when Baron Scicluna fractured my thumb. I wrestled for twenty minutes after it happened and I can recall how intense the pain was even in just a small area like that. There's no question...the Baron was tough.

Another rough customer was the Spaniard, Crusher Verdu...an exceptionally strong individual. He was only six feet one inch and weighed probably around 300 pounds. He wasn't fast and he didn't have the best stamina in the world, but he was famous for his backbreaking strength. Because he knew he didn't have the gas to last an hour in the ring, let alone the quickness to outmaneuver his challengers, he'd pour it on right from the first bell. He charged after you with full force and I'll bet 95% of his matches were won in the first seven or eight minutes.

Crusher realized that with me, he faced someone with strong stamina and good quickness. He felt that the only area in which he could challenge me and maybe come out the winner was to take me on in strength.

Our matches were never much to brag about when it came to showing off wrestling skills, but they were amazing as exhibitions of strength versus strength. And in the end, I always handled Crusher because my stamina would outlast his.

Once your stamina leaves, so does your strength. Without stamina, you can go from giant-killer to a helpless baby in a matter of minutes. That was Crusher Verdu's problem.

George Steele was another formidable opponent for me. I had some great matches with him. Most people today who see George Steele think they're watching some individual who's got a mental problem or they consider him mentally retarded. Well, they've got it all wrong.

When I wrestled George Steele years ago, he used to speak quite well for himself whenever he was interviewed. In point of fact, besides being a capable wrestler, George was a very bright man.

George Steele was always tough.

Do you know why George Steele has only wrestled on weekends and during the summer vacation season throughout most of his career? That's because he is an educator..an academic. He's taught at Michigan where his responsibilities have included wrestling coach and assistant football coach.

Yet people who have seen him wrestle in more recent years have the impression that he's just a new kid on the block who happens to weigh 300 pounds and who goes into the ring making faces and carrying on with a lot of nonsense.

Ah, then you have The Sheik. The Sheik's real name was Eddie Forhat and he was Syrian. Even though he had good wrestling skills, he chose not to use them most of the time. He was an unorthodox guy who did weird things in the ring that really threw you off guard.

The Sheik wasn't the type of wrestler with whom you felt you could pit your skills against and give the fans a match that could be appreciated. Instead, he would go in and out of the ring constantly. When he finally did step in to lock horns with you, just as fast he would just duck out under the ropes. He made having a legitimate bout very difficult.

I can honestly say I did not enjoy wrestling with The Sheik. Not that I

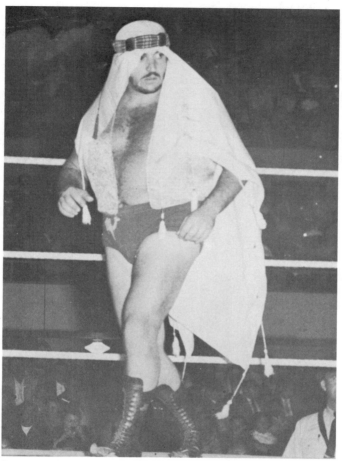

I never really enjoyed wrestling The Sheik.

had problems handling him in the ring, but it was because I didn't feel that I was giving the crowd the caliber of match that they had paid to see.

Ernie Ladd was a football powerhouse turned pro wrestler who surprised me. When he entered the profession, at six feet nine inches tall and weighing 320 pounds, even though he had some background in the sport, he didn't impress me as someone who had the potential skills that would make him into a headliner. I saw him as raw talent and nerve.

I have to say, to his credit, that he worked exceptionally hard and trained with many good people. He put football completely behind him and was determined to become the best wrestler he could be. At the time I'm speaking of, he was in his late 20's. To decide to become a pro at that late stage, I thought, was being very presumptuous.

But to his credit, he did what he set out to do. I must have wrestled him at least a dozen times or more and I really had to work for my victories against him. For a large guy, he was strong, well-coordinated with good speed.

I enjoyed our matches because they really were the kind of exhibitions that the fans truly enjoyed. I defended my title against Ladd a number of times and fortunately, did well against him.

Here I am being congratulated after one of my matches.

Of course, I can't forget about Crusher Lisowski. Depending on what part of the country you were from, you'd know about Crusher. Fans in Pennsylvania knew him well as did folks in Minneapolis and places further North where he made quite a name for himself.

Crusher was a burly barrel-chested guy, weighed about 250 pounds, who wore his blonde hair in an army crew cut. He talked in a rough tough voice that sounded like he'd swallowed razor blades. He was always in great shape and I understand he did a lot of road work along with weightlifting.

He was a real brawler who dished out as much as he took even though he didn't show much finesse with his moves. When I wrestled Lisowski, I knew that I'd been in a wrestling match.

Who else? Well, Bill Watts is certainly someone who I have vivid memories of. Bill was an amateur who came out of Oklahoma with an outstanding record. He stood six feet four inches tall and weighed over 300 pounds...big, raw-boned. Very strong and quick, he knew how to call on his skills from his amateur days. Because Watts was always in good shape, I wrestled some wars with him.

Bill and I had actually wrestled together as a tag team for a while, but that was going way, way back. I worked out with him in the gym, not only on the mat, but with the weights...and he could put the weight up, let me tell you.

I always took time to call my family when I was away.

97

Bill and I set some gate attendance records when we began to meet each other in head-to-head matches. Fans remembered that Bill and I had been tag team partners and that there had been a bit of a falling out. Watts had felt that by being my tag team partner, there was no way he was going to get his shot at my title. So to put himself in a better position for that, he broke away from our tag team arrangement. Watts was out to be Number One and the only way that could happen he felt was to take on Sammartino one-on-one and no longer work the tag team. After he cut himself loose, the promoters scrambled to line up his title shot, but he never beat me.

I should mention Gene Kiniski. Gene was a whirlwind, non-stop type of wrestler very similar to Kowalski. I can honestly say that to look at him, physically he wasn't the most impressive looking guy in the world, but he sure gave me some real tough nights.

Why? Because of his great stamina and aggressiveness. Kiniski also had the ability to take punishment and rebound from it in the wink of an eye. He was good enough to hold the National Wrestling Alliance title for several years. He went on to remain a tough contender for years before he quit the game.

During my Championship reign, as I just mentioned, there was a sister organization to the World Wide Wrestling Federation called the National Wrestling Alliance. The NWA held their own matches in their own territories and crowned their own Champion.

In the late 1960's, the NWA Champ was the Great Lou Thez, a man who was just an incredible technician in the ring. Of course, I was still the WWWF Champion.

Talks started to be generated concerning the unification of the two federations in April of 1969. First informally over the telephone, then in formal meetings in a number of different cities, Sam Mushnik, the president of the NWA, and Willie Gillzenberg, the president of the WWWF, along with Vince McMahon and Toots Mondt, initiated unification discussions. Typically enough, these meetings never involved myself or Thez who were the two reigning champions.

We didn't know what was going on, what rules were being discussed and if a unification title match was being cooked up. Finally, I was bold enough to ask Gillzenberg a direct question. I said, "Willie, you guys have met in St. Louis. You've met in Chicago. You've met in New York. What's holding everything up? I'm just as much a part of this as anyone else and I want to know what's happening. What are the problems here?"

Gillzenberg answered that all parties had come to an agreement that unification was going to take place. The one problem that remained was with the title match to be scheduled between Thez and me. Depending on who won that match, the promoters were concered about who was entitled to our services on what dates?

So once more the problem was who owned how much of what wrestler. Mc-Mahon had stated that he needed Bruno at least 17 days out of the month in order to fill the arenas he controlled. Sam Mushnik said that the NWA needed Bruno at least 16 days a month to make ends meet.

When I heard that this kind of drivel had brought negotiations to a standstill, I called for a meeting of my own. I asked Willie Gillzenberg, Phil Zacko who was also with the WWWF office, Vince McMahon and Kola Kwariani to meet with me in Washington, D.C. When the date was set, I hopped a plane from whatever part of the country I found myself in and came to the meeting.

An early portrait of NWA Champion Lou Thez.

I opened by saying, "You guys have been at all these meetings with the National Wrestling Alliance, talking non-stop about unification. Let me make this clear. There's nothing more than I'd like to do than to wrestle Lou Thez for the combined crown."

I'd wrestled Thez twice before...once to a draw and once he got a decision over me when I was just a rookie. Now the tide of time had turned and the advantage was with me, I thought. In 1969, I'd been a champion over six years and Thez, who was much older than I was, had begun to slow down. I wanted to wrestle him again because I felt that now I could finally beat him.

I said to the men at the meeting and particularly to Vince McMahon, "I believe I will win this match with Thez. But the match doesn't even matter to you. You people are discussing who gets Bruno sixteen days and who gets Bruno fifteen days. And what it all means is from the time this unification happens, I'll be wrestling seven days a week, 52 weeks out of the year."

"Let me tell you gentlemen, if you can't get your heads together and work out a way where you'll wrestle me 25 or 26 days a month, then I won't be a part of it. I need time off...not only for health reasons but for family purposes, too. I don't get a chance to see my family at all right now...and the schedule you're suggesting is going to be even worse."

"So let me caution you that as you continue to have your unification meetings, don't argue about who gets Bruno for sixteen days and who gets Bruno for fifteen days. Argue instead about who's going to get Bruno for twelve days and who's going to get Bruno for eleven days...because I will not accept a title match if you men make any other arrangement." I concluded my remarks, thanked them all for coming and left.

I found out later that the WWWF contingent had one more meeting of their own. Somebody, and to this day I don't know who, got up and said "Why bother with unification at all? We got Bruno and he's such a star attraction that he's filling all of our arenas anyway. With unification, that means only one thing. We're going to have less of him to go around and how is that going to benefit the WWWF?"

That was the argument that carried the day. They decided not to unify and they called me once again. They told me that they took into consideration everything that I had to say and that they had decided to scrap plans for the unification with the NWA. And that was that.

Before I close this chapter, let me tell you about one man that I wanted to wrestle, but never got the opportunity to do so. That was Andre the Giant. Now I'm talking about a young Andre, when he was such a force in the late 60's and early 70's.

In those days, Andre stood over seven feet tall and weighed around 450 pounds. He could really move and do fantastic things in the ring. Since then he's put on over 100 pounds and in my opinion, is just a shadow of his

100

That's bodybuilder turned actor Arnold Schwarzenegger on my left.

former self.

When I first saw Andre perform, I said I wanted to take him on. So I went to Vince McMahon and told him "Vince, since I'm world champion, I think it's important to work toward a match between me and Andre the Giant. He's making quite a name for himself and he deserves it. I just don't think it looks good for me not to defend my title against such a strong opponent."

"Besides," I went on, "it's a match made in heaven. It'll be a great box office draw. What's also important is to show the world that anybody who deserves a crack at the title will get it."

McMahon was shaking his head all the while I was talking. He said finally, "This whole thing's been brought up to me before. I've thought about it but it's no go. Here's why...Andre the Giant is unique because of his size. What that means is that you can't keep him tied down to one territory. You got to keep moving him around the country because believe me, once people see a guy like that in the same arena time after time, the novelty wears off fast. And one thing more, Bruno...whether you won the match or Andre wins the match, the WWWF loses either way."

I didn't follow his logic. "Explain that one to me, Vince."

Awaiting my opponent to enter the ring.

"Simple," McMahon answered. "If you beat him, then that's the end of Andre. He'll no longer be the eighth wonder of the world. We've been promoting him by saying he's unbeatable. You beat him and that kills him off right there. And if Andre beats you, as champion he'll not draw. There just aren't that many opponents that could stand up to him and that the fans would pay to see. And you'd be hurt by it because in the eyes of the fans you're no longer the best because Andre the Giant had conquered you.

I disagreed. "That's not the way to look at it. I think I can really beat the man. I've beaten bigger men than him. Calhoun was almost 200 pounds heavier and I beat him. I wrestled a guy in Singapore they called King Kong and I beat him. He weighed over 500 pounds. Just give the chance. I can do it."

McMahon said that he would think it over, but he never went through with the match. Since McMahon held Andre's contract and since Andre himself never showed any interest in wrestling with me, the match never materialized.

Too bad. Who knows how it might have turned out.

LOSING, WINNING AND LEARNING

On January 8, 1968, our twin sons were born. Their names are Danny and Darryl. Because of the hardships that Carol had to undergo during her first delivery of David, we were so happy that everything went well this time. When they were born, I had promised myself that I wouldn't be away as much and as often as 1 had been with David. It wasn't until 1971 that I got the chance to really keep that promise.

At home with my twins.

The circumstances that brought about my opportunity to spend more time at home certainly didn t come about by desire or intention on my part. Let me tell you what happened.

By the end of 1970 and into the early weeks of 1971, I had been champion for over seven and a half years. My schedule had been grueling because I'd been on a six and seven day work week for all of that period. And I'd had injuries all along the way...the elbows, the ribs, fingers, knees and back. You name it and I had it...cuts, scrapes, contusions, sprains, strains and breaks.

Unfortunately, I was never able to afford the luxury of taking time to let myself heal properly. I hurtled on with my career and in the process, I met many, many tough opponents. Each one took their toll on my body.

Then, I agreed to wrestle a guy that I had defeated a number of times before...Ivan Koloff. Every match with Koloff was an all-out war and in fact, I enjoyed wrestling him because he was so good.

His nickname was the Russian Bear and he had the strength and the lightning quick moves of a grizzly. Ivan stood about six feet tall and weighed around 300 hundred pounds. He was always in great shape, had exceptional stamina and was very strong.

Even though I had been successful against him in all of my previous matches, as the saying goes, "On any given night, anybody can beat anybody." On this particular night, January 18, 1971, the match was going good...a typical Sammartino and Koloff bout.

We had packed the fans into Madison Square Garden. It had been a complete sell-out with thousands of people turned away at the gates..and the fans inside were getting their money's worth.

I remember I was coming off the ropes and I positioned myself for his counter-move, but Koloff fooled me. He caught me with a knee that cut me on the side of my head. I was dazed badly by the blow.

Koloff rushed at me, scooped me up and gave me a powerful body slam, then punctuated that with a knee drop across my throat. As I struggled to move, Koloff scrambled up onto the top rope and hurled himself down into me, driving another knee across my chest.

As quick as a flash of dynamite, he covered me. As I tried desperately to get up, the referee slammed his palm into the canvas three times. I was counted out. Koloff was the victor and the new world's heavyweight champion of professional wrestling. He had beaten me for the first time...and that was all it took.

I pulled myself up off the mat and for a second it wasn't clear to me what had happened. I thought at first that something was wrong with my ears. I couldn't hear a sound!

Here I was in the middle of Madison Square Garden with 21,500 fans looking on. All I heard was silence. What had Koloff's barrage done to me?

I looked back and forth across the faces of the fans, trying to make sense of everything. Then I realized what had happened. The people were just sitting there in a state of shock! No one could believe that Bruno Sammartino had lost the match. The whole Garden was as quiet as a tomb.

Then I started hearing little cries, whimpers. Talk about emotional moments, this was one that really got to me.

I heard sobbing. I heard cries. Someone called out, "Bruno, you're still the best! We love you, Bruno!"

As I stepped out of the ring and walked back to my dressing room, fans reached out to pat me on the back or to touch my robe. I heard someone say, "You'll be back, Bruno! Don't worry, we all love you!"

I got very choked up about what the fans were saying to me as I left the floor of the Garden. They had given me such great support all through the years and even though I had lost my title that night, they stood by me.

In the dressing room, many different people came around to console me...promoters, other wrestlers. Of course, the media came asking questions. How did I feel now that I had lost? What were my plans now? Was I going to retire?

Eventually the dressing room cleared and I was left to my own thoughts. I remembered being in this same dressing room nearly eight years ago, when I had just won the title and how strong had been my sense of pride and how great had been my feelings of responsibility to my fans. This night though I felt a great sadness. Perhaps I had let them all down...the fans, my family, the promoters.

Then a new feeling came over me. I actually started to feel good about my possibilities. I had put in my time, and my financial situation was certainly not the same as it had been in those early days. I had my home, my financial security and my family.

I started to think, "Hey, maybe this whole thing is going to be okay... because now I can go home and spend time with my family. Now I can allow the aches and pains from all the nights of pounding start to heal."

I began to accept my defeat. I began to see positive things coming out of my loss.

The next day I had no place to go but home. All the dates that I had been signed for were for the new champion to fill. It was now up to Ivan Koloff to defend his crown.

I caught a plane and went home. When I arrived, Carol and the rest of my family thought I would be devastated. Instead, they saw a happy, almost jubilant guy come home. And I know that deep down inside, they too were happy when they realized that I would be with my family from now on.

My wife Carol and I attend one of many functions.

108

I really just wanted to heal. For about a month, I didn't do anything. I decided to be good to myself and I quit training so as not to put any type of stress on any part of my body. After a while, I started feeling much better.

After those four weeks, I went back to training. Guess I couldn't live without it.

Then to my surprise, offers started coming in from promoters all over the country. Now that I was free from having to defend my title, dates started opening up for me.

I thought, "Look at this...I'm no longer the champion and still everybody is calling me."

I said to myself, "Okay...I'll take all the additional time I need to heal up properly, train hard, then go from there."

I scheduled bouts at my own pace, far enough apart so that in a week I would only wrestle perhaps twice. That was certainly a far cry from the old days where sometimes a week equaled seven work days. I started traveling to places like St. Louis for a match, then I'd go off to California, or I'd bounce over to Tennessee, Florida and New York.

Vince McMahon still booked me, too, on behalf of the WWWF and he'd have me appearing in Philadelphia and at Madison Square Garden once in a blue moon. Then the promoters in Japan would call me and I'd say I couldn't commit for three weeks but I'd agree to one week. And then I'd book myself for two weeks of relaxation after I'd get back from the Far East. All in all I was really enjoying my life immensely at this point because I got to spend much more time at home.

110

Enjoying the fruits of my labor.

This life style lasted nearly two years from January of 1971 to December of 1973. Then just when I least expected it, Lady Luck had other things in mind for me.

I had agreed to travel to Japan for ten days, starting the last week in November of '73. Just before I left, McMahon called me up, sounding desperate. He said he had a weak card scheduled for Madison Square Garden on December the 10th. He was really concerned about it because he didn't have a strong main event. What Vince wanted was for me to wrestle Stan Stasiak, an up-and-coming young talent. He thought that pairing us would solve his problems about filling the Garden.

I didn't really want to accept this match since it was too close to my return from Japan. I would be back around December 7th and the Garden appearance would be only three days later. But Vince pleaded with me so I said okay, reluctantly.

What happened next was an amazing chain of events that got to be unbelievable. On the day I left for Japan, Stan Stasiak wrestled the then reigning champion of the WWWF, Pedro Morales. And Stasiak beat Morales. He whipped him and now he owned the belt.

So when I came back from the Far East ten days later, I find out that I had returned for a title match. Now Bruno Sammartino was going to wrestle Stan Stasiak for the title!

I posed with McMahon, Sr. and Pedro Morales before I left for Japan.

I really hadn't expected to be wrestling for the title.

The Garden was sold out. Fans came from all over to witness the championship match. I heard the people chanting again, "Bruno! Bruno" and I said to myself, "My God, I can't let them down. I've got to go out there and win this match.''

Then I thought, ''But wait a minute. If I win, that means I'm champion again. The whole grind would start right up.''

The title was the last thing I wanted, but what was I to do? If I beat Stasiak for the fans, then I got the belt back. If I lost to Stasiak, then I disappointed the fans again.

The match turned out to be a great one. Stasiak was a good, tough wrestler. We went at it, tooth and nail, for twenty five minutes...and I won. I pinned him and all of a sudden Bruno Sammartino was back on top again. The ex-champion had become the new champion.

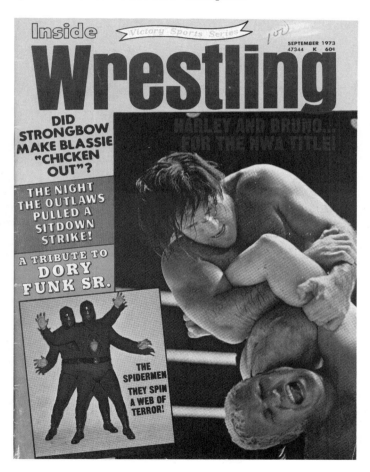

Despite the fact that I had won, I wasn't the happiest fellow in the world at that point. I had been spoiled for the last couple of years, enjoying wrestling because I was doing it at my own pace, going to places that I wanted to and spending lots of time at home with my family.

When I took the title back, letters poured in, congratulating me. People would stop me on the street, in stores, everywhere and pound me on the back and say, "Atta boy, Bruno!" And I would smile and thank them for their kind words.

But in reality, I didn't feel all that great about it because only I knew what lay ahead. The grind. The same old grind.

When I first captured the title in '63, my attitude was, "Thank God! Winning is going to change my life. It's going to help me do all the things I've wanted to do."

The second time around I realized what a burden I had shackled myself to. Not that I wasn't grateful for all the fan support but I had been going GREAT without it. Maybe I would pull in more money again, but only I knew what lay ahead of me. The ridiculous schedule and not seeing my family for long stretches. If I had known that it would continue for four more years, I might have felt even more depressed about it.

From that night on December 10th, 1973 until 1977, my career took off again. Despite my misgivings, when I went back into the ring, I wrestled with the same energy that I had when I was just coming up. The fan support just boosted me sky-high. I would go into arenas and hear 20,000 people chanting, 'Bruno! Bruno! Bruno!' and that would energize me every time.

I would never do anything to let the fans down. If I ever had a bad match, it certainly wasn't from my lack of effort. I always gave it everything I had. And like my first reign, there were many, many tough opponents who gave everything they had right back to me!

Some names that come to mind include Don Leo Jonathan. Don Leo was mammoth, six feet eight and 330 pounds and one of the most feared wrestlers in the business. His father, Deacon Jonathan, had been a great wrestler in the 30's and 40's and those wrestling skills definitely ran in the family. Don Leo had been a top-ranked amateur who came highly touted to professional wrestling. He was a tough opponent and for a giant, he did things that were unheard of...like flips and back somersaults!

I wrestled Don Leo many times and he almost gave me an inferiority complex because I was supposed to have been the stronger wrestler. I could remember in the Sixties that I was regarded as the strongest wrestler in the world. By this time in the Seventies, I even started questioning my own strength...especially when I went up against Jonathan. This guy would pick

I always tried to sign autographs for my fans as much as possible.

I wrestled Don Leo many times.

me up and throw me around like I was a feather.

I respected him because he had just about everything in his package...great strength, solid wrestling skills and incredible agility. I would put him in the same class as Killer Kowalski, Ivan Koloff, Gorilla Monsoon or the Japanese giant, Tanaka.

Another wrestler I especially recall from my second reign was Ken Patera. Ken had been a standout at Portland and was considered one of the best all-around athletes ever to compete at the college level. I mean he had it all. He excelled in track events like the shotput and the discus. He was a weightlifter who went to the Olympics twice for the United States. He could

116

have had a professional career in football if he had chosen to do so.

I remember one particular match with Patera where he must have slammed me from post to post ten times. He was incredibly strong and let's face it, by the time I had reached my late 30's, I had lost a step or two.

On my own behalf, although I was no longer considered the strongest wrestler around, I was still a force to be reckoned with. I still had plenty of strength left, though maybe not like before, and my stamina was always there. You just couldn't wear me out.

Another tactic that I had taken to make up for losing that step was to drop nearly twenty-five pounds. I went from 275 pounds down to 250 pounds and wrestled at that weight during the better part of my second championship.

One wrestler who never received the proper recognition was Bobby Duncam. I wrestled him quite a few times in the Seventies and I was always impressed with his performance.

Bobby had wrestled as an amateur at Texas A & M and had played football there, too. After college, at first he tried a professional stint as a lineman for the St. Louis Cardinals. Back then, pro football wasn't paying much for a lineman's services and Bobby found out you could make a lot more money in professional wrestling. He dumped football after a couple of frustrating years and went on to dedicate himself completely to wrestling.

I had some of the greatest matches in my career against Bobby Duncam. Now he might not have necessarily been my greatest opponent, but he certainly gave me all I could handle.

I'll tell you...Bobby was quick and had a vast knowledge of the game. And he brought a sense of timing with him into the ring that was phenomenal. Now I've wrestled so many of the great ones and in my opinion, Bobby Duncam stands in tall with all of them. Yet he is the least known of the bunch. Nobody wrote much about him. Nobody ever recognized his skills to any extent. I think he was a lot better competitor than many of those wrestlers who grabbed the headlines and hogged the cameras.

The one guy that I certainly remember most vividly was Stan Hansen, not for his wrestling skills particularly but for what happened in the ring with him. He broke my neck!

There have been all kinds of ridiculous stories written about how Hansen broke my neck with a lariat. That's all those stories are...just nonsense.

Hansen was a big man, six feet four or so, weighing in around 310 pounds. And he was green, a real rookie. People might say that I didn't take him seriously, but that's not the case. I always took everyone seriously and was always on my guard.

On this night, April 25th, 1976, we were going at a pretty furious pace for nearly fifteen minutes. I'm looking at Hansen and thinking, "Boy, this guy is out of gas already!"

It was obvious he was tired. The fact was that Hansen, a young man in his twenties, just didn't have the stamina that I still had in my thirties.

I started coming off the ropes and catching him with tackles. Then it happened. He tried to scoop me up for a body slam and he didn't have the strength left in his arms to execute it properly. He got me up in the air, but couldn't handle my weight to bodyslam me onto my back. Instead, Hansen dropped me...dropped me right on top of my head...and the neck broke.

It was like I had taken a bolt of lightning through my body. I nearly blacked out and yet the match continued. Nobody knew that my neck had snapped and we kept wrestling for a few more minutes. I was operating on pure instinct alone.

Stan Hansen & Fred Blassie

Then, Hansen made an attempt at a second bodyslam and got caught using an illegal hold while he was trying to pull off the slam. The referee charged in and disqualified Hansen and only then was the match halted. From that point on, all I remembered were flashing red lights and an ambulance siren. The pain had put me out.

After the match, I was rushed by ambulance to a hospital in New York. Ringside people suspected that something very serious was wrong. I heard later that the State Athletic Commissioner himself had attended the match and when I was dropped on my head, he turned to his companion and said, "My God, that man's been seriously hurt."

I had absolutely no feeling on one side. The rest of me was in excruciating pain.

Bernard Spiegle, a friend of mine who's also my tax attorney in New York, would always come to the Garden and watch me whenever I was in town. Usually after the show, Bernie and I would go to my favorite Italian restaurant in the city, Delsomme, which some dear friends of mine from Sicily, the Cardinale Brothers, had opened. There was no Old Country cuisine the night I broke my neck though.

Bernie rode with me in the ambulance. As I fought through the waves of pain, I kept thinking about my wife. I knew how frightened she was going to be when she heard about my injury.

And I worried about my parents. They were both in their 80's then and I mumbled to Bernie, "My God, if my parents hear that their son is in a New York City hospital with a serious injury, there will be two heart attacks in Pittsburgh."

After we arrived at the hospital and I was examined, the doctors told me that I was to stay put. They didn't want me to move another inch until they could figure out what they wanted to do with me.

I tried to talk to Bernie, tried to make sense. "Bernie, I know why they don't want me to leave the hospital. They just don't want to be responsible for what might happen to me. Tell them that I have to take that risk. I've got to get back home. Tell them to get a release from my doctor in Pittsburgh."

Then the fog rolled in on me. Somebody, probably Bernie, dialed my wife for me. I got on the phone and I tried not to scare her. I told her that I got hurt in the match tonight, that I was at a New York hospital, but I was going to come home as soon as I could get a consent release from my own personal doctor. She sounded shaken up by my news, but she said she'd take care of it.

Carol then called Doctor Louis Civitarese, my physician for many, many years. I had met Doc Civitarese in Pittsburgh at ringside because he was the State Athletic Commission doctor and attended all the matches in that capacity. I found out that he was a surgeon at Divine Providence Hospital and had gotten involved with wrestling as a hobby. He loved athletics. I trusted him completely and he always took wonderful care of me.

In a short while, Doc Civitarese was on the line, asking me what had happened. After I told him, he said that he was willing to fly to New York to attend to me. I told him no. I said that I had to come back to Pittsburgh so as not to upset my parents and that he had to tell the doctors here that it was okay for me to do that.

Finally, Doc Civitarese agreed after I assured him that I could travel and would be all right. He talked to the New York doctors and I was released into his hands. Bernie took me to the airport and saw me onto the plane.

I cannot even hope to describe what my flight was like from New York to Pittsburgh. The pain continued to explode in me. Any movement just made everything worse. Bar none, it was the most incredible journey I think I ever made.

I remember when I arrived at Divine Providence in Pittsburgh, Doc Civitarese took one look at me and his face flushed. He was extremely angry with me and he proceeded to chew me out in no uncertain terms. He said, "Bruno, don't you understand what kind of injury you have?" I had no idea.

"Don't you understand that the slightest little bump or jerk or movement and the broken bone in your neck will cut into your spinal cord? And when that happens you're either dead or paralyzed from the neck down!"

After getting over his initial shock at seeing me, Doc gathered his troops together, talking to his top neurosurgeon and his top orthopedic man. Through it all, it was clear that Doc Civitarese was totally in charge.

The next morning my sister Mary came to the hospital with my folks. I had asked my sister to bring them there as soon as she could before they overheard all sorts of wild stories on the news. She had briefed them as gently as possible that I had had an accident while wrestling in New York and that I was now resting comfortably in the hospital in Pittsburgh.

Actually, reports of my injury were all over the television stations the night I came back. Fortunately, my parents went to bed before the eleven o'clock news so they had missed all the reports, Thank God.

Both my brother and sister were worried that all the paisans would have heard the news and start to call my parents' home early in the morning asking, "How's Bruno? My God, how is he?" Of course, they would think that Mom and Dad would already have known. Fortunately, that didn't happen either.

When they walked into my hospital room and saw the Doctor there with all of his assistants, my parents started to get all shook up. My Mom was really scared that I'd been badly hurt. But we all played it as though what had happened to me wasn't all that significant. That was the way I wanted it.

You know, after they went home later, they did start to get calls from friends and relatives from all over. They told everyone that their son was going to be okay...that it was all right. I'm not sure that Mom and Dad ever were really aware of the seriousness of my injury...and that's good.

I found out later that the media bombarded the hospital with requests to get an interview with me, but it was no dice. Doctor Civitarese laid down the law, "No interviews! Not in his condition!"

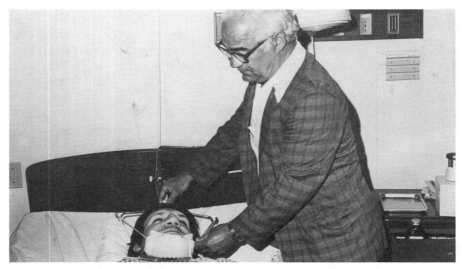

Doc Civitarese adjusts my Miami Brace.

Later in the day after my parents were gone, one of the specialists, the neurosurgeon, told me straight, "Bruno, I'm afraid that you will never be able to go back to wrestling. You've had your career and now that's over. You're finished with wrestling."

Then Doctor Best, who had been an orthopedic surgeon for the Pittsburgh Steelers, came to my room and sang a different tune. He said, "Athletes are strange birds, Bruno. What might be a crippling injury for an ordinary person is not necessarily the same for an athlete. I've seen athletes come back from some extremely serious injuries...injuries that have amazed me."

122

Best leveled with me. "Yours is a very serious injury. I don't know if you are interested in returning to wrestling, but I'm not going to rule it out for you. I'm not going to give you the gloom and doom approach like the others you've been hearing. Recovery may take time, but it is a possibility."

Even though the neurosurgeon had said I was through, here was another expert telling me I had a chance. As for Doc Civitarese, he wasn't committing himself one way or the other. He knew how serious my condition was and he also knew how I had recuperated from other injuries before. His approach was one of wait and see.

While I was flat on my back in the hospital, the world of professional wrestling kept churning. International promoters were putting together a match between Mohammad Ali and the great Japanese wrestler Antonio Inoki. Yes, that's right. They were setting up a fighter versus wrestler bout.

In fact, Vince McMahon had attempted to get Ali and me into a similar match prior to the Ali/Inoki pairing. McMahon couldn't come up with the $6 million dollars that Ali wanted so my shot at Ali went by the boards.

But Vince's idea intrigued the Inoki backers in Japan and the promoters there were able to get the Ali/Inoki match off the ground. It was to be fought in Japan and shown simultaneously all over the world on closed circuit television.

McMahon still wanted a piece of this action so he went into partnership with Bob Arum, who was doing the major promotion for it. McMahon committed himself for a large amount of money to obtain the closed circuit rights throughout the Northeastern Region.

But the bout just wasn't moving. It was kind of eerie because there was no reaction to it from the fans. Nothing.

McMahon got very worried that if the match didn't go, then it was curtains for him since he had a ton of money on the line. He would be facing bankruptcy...pure and simple.

So, while I'm laying there in the hospital bed, with tubes running this way and that, and with all these instruments hooked up, Vince called me. Since I couldn't hold the phone, the Nurse held the receiver up to my ear.

He went straight to the point. "Bruno, I'm going to be dead...finished. This Ali and Inoki match isn't drawing flies. I need you to bail me out. Let me make a match between you and Stan Hansen. We'll have it at Shea Stadium and put it on closed circuit along with the Ali bout. Your match'll be the one the fans pay to see and that'll save my butt."

All I could say to him was, "Vince, I don't know. I'm so banged up I can hardly talk let alone walk. Nobody knows what I'm going to be like in a couple of months."

But Vince kept pestering me, calling me day after day, trying to talk me into signing for a match at the same time I was hospitalized with a broken neck. You had to know Vince to realize what the man was capable of.

When Doc Civitarese got wind that Vince McMahon was calling me constantly about a possible match, he got really ticked off about it. Everybody did. Even my wife, Carol.

She said, "Bruno, you better not even think about it. Vince isn't concerned about you at all. He's only out for himself."

That was true to a degree. What Vince was telling was that his business was in deep trouble and he needed a miracle to salvage a serious situation.

Once Doc Civitarese came in during one of Vince's calls. He grabbed the phone from the Nurse who was holding it for me and he screamed into the receiver. "Is this Mister McMahon? Well, Mister McMahon, I'm Doctor Louis Civitarese and I'm taking care of Bruno. I just want you to get one thing clear. Bruno is suffering from a broken neck. He is extremely lucky to be alive and in fact, he came within a millimeter of being paralyzed from the neck down. As far as Bruno being able to wrestle again, that's to be determined way down the road. Now, Mister McMahon, before I hang up, let me ask you never to call Bruno again." And Doc slammed the phone down on Vince's ear.

But even that kind of treatment didn't influence McMahon to back off. The next time he called, the first thing he said to me was, "Don't ever put that last guy on the phone again. I don't want to talk to him."

So Vince kept calling and we kept talking. Finally, Vince came up with another scheme. "Look, Bruno. If we can at least make the announcement about your match with Hansen, say six weeks before it's scheduled, that would save me."

I answered quickly, "I don't want you to make an announcement and then I can't do it. That would make it even worse for you in the long run."

McMahon shot back, 'I'm not worried about you not making it. Let's face the facts here. This guy Hansen is a rulebreaker. Everything he does is illegal. So let's take this a step further. We book the match and it's happening. The first time that this guy throws an illegal blow, the referee will disqualify him. Believe me, we're not going to take any chances with your health. But again, we need you in that match to save the organization or otherwise we're in deep, deep trouble."

I took a deep breath and said, "Okay, Vince. Go ahead and make your announcement."

Of course, when my family and Doc Civitarese heard what I had done, they were all furious with me. They couldn't believe that I would risk such a match. But I told them that it was something I had to do. There was too much at stake not to risk it.

Finally after about a month, I was released from Divine Providence. Then for another month after that, I had to wear this ridiculous device that the therapists had rigged up called the Miami Brace. It was a steel contraption that fastened like a belt at the waist. It also had support bars that ran out from the waistband. One came up under my chin and the other one ran around back to support my neck. There were knobs that you could tighten or loosen to make the brace more or less comfortable. I was supposed to keep this thing on at all times. Well, at least I wore it all the way home.

Then shortly after I get home, Vince tells me that he's lined up a television interview for me on Channel Eleven and that now is the perfect time to make the announcement about my match. I made the trip to the station and got on the air and said that I was out to make things right between me and the guy who inflicted this injury on me. And that was that. The match was officially on.

I started doing some light training at home and I do mean light. I really didn't want to put any kind of stress on my neck. I worked to tighten up muscles that had gone flat from laying around in the hospital.

When the date got nearer for the match with Hansen, the State Athletic Commission stepped in and said that they weren't going to allow it until they examined me and certified me fit. This worried me a little bit because I thought they might turn me down.

I flew to New York for the examination. Doc Civitarese was still angry with me for moving ahead with the match. He wanted to come to New York to be there when I was examined, but as it turned out, another one of his patients became seriously ill. He had to perform emergency surgery and couldn't come. Ironic the way things happen.

Well, I passed my physical and Commissioner Foy himself gave his approval for the match to proceed. I do know that Commissioner Foy was a strict man with the rules and that if the Commission's doctor had said no, then it would have been no.

As it happened, the match between Mohammed Ali and Antonio Inoki was a complete bomb...a total disaster. I don't even think Inoki's mother watched it. On the other hand, wherever my match with Stan Hansen went out on closed circuit, fans flocked to see it and paid good money to do so.

Our match was piggy-backed with the Ali/Inoki debacle...and it also took place on that same evening. That night when I went into the ring with Stan Hansen, I wasn't exactly sure at first how I was going to handle him. He was a big, tough guy and I still owned this serious injury. I decided that the

WORLD MARTIAL ARTS CHAMPIONSHIP
FRIDAY, JUNE 25TH, 1976
WORLD HEAVYWEIGHT CHAMPION BOXER VS. TOP JAPANESE HEAVYWEIGHT WRESTLER

MUHAMMAD ALI

ANTONIO INOKI

AMERICAN REVOLUTION BICENTENNIAL 1776-1976

OFFICIAL PROGRAM - 75¢

IIII Spectrum

(215) FU 9-5000 PHILADELPHIA 19148

Star · Spangled Spectrum

AMERICAN REVOLUTION BICENTENNIAL 1776-1976

BRUNO SAMMARTINO VS.

STAN HANSEN

NO. 52

THE OFFICIAL PROGRAM OF THE
WORLD WIDE WRESTLING FEDERATION

W.W.W.F. CHAMPIONSHIP
WRESTLING

THE WORLD WIDE
WRESTLING FEDERATION
W.W.W.F.
WILLIE GILZENBERG,
PRESIDENT

best way I could beat him was at his own game...attack...go for the advantage immediately. After all, I remembered our last match. Hansen had broken my neck with an illegal maneuver.

That's what I did. I attacked him with a vengeance almost like a villain. I was determined to survive this match at all costs. I did what I had to do. Whether or not I would be disqualified never entered my mind. All I cared about was not getting hurt. I wanted to hurt him instead of him hurting me again.

I admit I didn't use my best wrestling knowledge and to be truthful, I shouldn't have been in there in the first place. It was way too soon for a comeback.

For me, justice prevailed. I won my rematch with Stan Hansen and had some small measure of revenge for him breaking my neck. After that, I decided I desperately needed to take some time off to continue the healing. And that's what I did.

As a sidebar to the Hansen match, McMahon ended up only paying me out of the receipts from the Shea Stadium gate. I had no contract, only a gentlemen's agreement. Consequently, I didn't get a dime from any of the closed circuit revenues.

When I confronted McMahon about that, I said, "Vince, I came back with a broken neck to bail you out of your misery and now you're telling me there's no money from the closed circuit telecast!"

McMahon said, "There's not much I can do for you, Bruno. I can't really give you anything from the closed circuit because I don't have the say on that. That part of the deal is controlled by the other promoters. Sorry."

So I was paid ten per cent from the Shea Stadium receipts and McMahon stayed in business. Would it be an understatement to say that I felt cheated?

THE BEAT GOES ON

The year 1977 rolled around and by this time I was down to around 245 pounds. Even though I no longer carried the 275 pounds that I weighed throughout most of my career, I still felt I was as strong if not stronger than most wrestlers out there.

Even so, by now I had started to talk about retirement, but it seemed like I was always talked out of it. The promoters kept telling me, "Why should you retire, Bruno? You're still in great shape...still one of the best in the business."

Being introduced at one of my many matches.

And other wrestlers would say to me, "Why retire? You're still at the top of your game...your injuries are healed."

What everyone didn't know of course was that every time I climbed into the ring, the neck would bother me. Other injuries to my back that I'd suffered over the years were starting to have a cumulative effect. Then there were some shoulder and leg problems that were now getting my attention.

What worried me the most was the nagging feeling of not quite being able to execute the great wrestling moves for which I was so well known throughout the Sixties. There was no question...these injuries were taking their toll.

I was getting a little self-conscious about myself and my abilities. I realized too that new fans were always popping up and I didn't want them to see a guy who had been the best in the world in the 1960's now not performing up to that level. I was very conscious of the fans' demand for excellence so I pushed all the harder.

In 1977, Super Star Billy Graham had one of the finest physiques in professional wrestling. I wrestled and defeated Graham many times. With him, matches would get down to pitting strength against strength. You couldn't say that he was a brawler either, but Billy just didn't use a lot of wrestling moves. I don't know whether he lacked the technical knowledge or if he just simply wanted to turn bouts into tests of strength. I never had what I'd call a great match with him as far as showing the fans good wrestling maneuvers.

Nevertheless, on April 30th, 1977 at the Civic Center in Baltimore, Maryland, Graham defeated me in a match and became the new heavyweight wrestling champion. He went on to hold the title for nine months, certainly making his mark in professional wrestling.

Let me tell you how it happened. Throughout most of the match, I held the advantage over Graham. He was hurt and bleeding pretty badly when I got him against a corner and I was really doing a good number on him. Then the referee pushed me away for a second and Graham went down almost to one knee. As I was coming at him again, Graham hooked my leg, tripped me and took me down to the mat.

That predicament would normally have been no problem for me to escape from, but then he covered me and while the referee got down to count, Graham threw both of his feet against the steel post for support. With that illegal advantage, he held me down long enough for the referee to count one, two, three and I was out. I lost the match and the title under those circumstances.

Films that we watched later clearly showed Graham's feet braced against

the post, but the Commissioners were not about to reverse a referee's ver-
dict. It was an injustice to be sure but I hope I don't sound like just a sore

Superstar Billy Graham and I do battle.

loser. Even though I felt that it was a bad way to lose the title, I thought it wasn't a very honorable way to win one either.

In fact as fate would have it, nine months later Billy Graham lost his title under virtually the same circumstances. Graham was up against Bob Backlund and Backlund had Billy under control with his shoulders down, waiting for the referee to count Billy out. Just as the count reached two, Graham realized that he wasn't going to be able to spring free in time, so he threw his leg over the bottom rope. The only problem was that the referee didn't see this, finished the count and Graham was beaten.

In a way, Billy Graham lost his title the same way that he had won it. Maybe the old adage rings true. You live by the sword, you die by the sword.

After I lost the title to Graham, I again began seriously considering retirement. By now, I had proven my point to everybody. I could come back and wrestle again...even from such an injury as a broken neck.

Even before the Graham bout, I had my reasons to continue. I certainly didn't want to hear for the rest of my life on television and in all the wrestling magazines that Stan Hansen was the man who retired Bruno Sammartino. I wanted to come back and kill that story so I wrestled for a good long while after my recovery and defended my title numerous times.

So now it's post-Graham and once more I'm faced with the retirement question. And again, the promoters and my fellow pros argued with me. Why quit when you still have the skills to keep winning?

McMahon said, "Bruno, just go for a few more years. You're still young...I mean young for your years."

What his backhanded compliment meant was that he still considered me in good shape and here I was, in my early forties. Actually, I had trimmed down a little bit more. My neck still was giving me problems, but I would never admit this to anyone.

So after the Graham bout, I thought I might as well keep going until I get a chance to think about everything more seriously. I cut down again on the number of matches I would accept, traveling occasionally to places like Los Angeles, St. Louis or Boston. And you know what? I was very happy working at this pace and I continued on that way for nearly three more years.

One interesting sidelight to my career happened in 1978 when Vince suggested that I take up the role of television color commentator. That challenge intrigued me so I agreed to do it.

I would sit at the announcer's table to comment on the other matches on the card...or sometimes I would do programs where my only function was to add my two cents worth to the proceedings. For a while I had a blast doing this but finally after two years I gave up the microphone.

In February, 1980, the decision to retire finally came to me. I had been on a tour of Texas, going to cities like Dallas, Houston, Amarillo and Lubbock and on a side excursion to Albuquerque, New Mexico. I can't say where or when it hit me, but I knew that it was time to call it quits professionally. I'm sure I could have gone on even longer, but the point was, why not retire? Maybe I started to think a little about Primo Carnera and Gorgeous George's last days in the ring and I sure knew I didn't want to go out that way.

When I came back from the conclusion of this tour, McMahon had slated me for a TV appearance. I had made up my mind that I was going to tell McMahon about my wishes. I was going to name the specific date when my retirement would begin and I thought that the TV appearance would be the perfect forum for my announcement. Once again, fate stepped in to change my plans.

It was around this time that I broke a young wrestler into the business by the name of Larry Zbyszko. Larry was a Pittsburgher who was a fantastic amateur wrestler. I first met him in 1970 when he was wrestling for North Allegheny High School. He compiled a tremendous record and wanted to turn pro right out of High School.

I suggested that it would be best for his career if he'd go earn a college degree first and keep developing his wrestling skills at the college level. I told him if he did that, then I would help him become a pro. But l would not help him if he tried to turn pro after graduating from High School. I had talked to his parents about this and they definitely agreed with me. They also wanted Larry to go on to college.

Larry did his four years at college, and he came back to me and said, "Look, you had promised to help me get into professional wrestling if I went to college. Well, I did. Now I'm ready to turn pro. How about showing me what it takes?"

Okay, I said and so I began working out with Larry quite a bit. I would bring in other wrestlers that I knew to give him all sorts of different competition. No question that Larry Zbyszko was an extremely talented athlete.

Finally, I felt he was good enough to hit the road. I called up a couple of promoters that I knew and they booked him right away. Larry went off to wrestle in Vancouver, British Columbia where he stayed for quite some time. Then the promoters moved him back to the States after he had picked up considerable experience and he went to places in Florida, Georgia...all over the South actually.

Of course, I kept in touch with Larry as much as I could. A few times he was booked in Pittsburgh. I went to see him work and believe me, I was even more impressed. I talked to McMahon about checking Larry out. I told Vince that this new kid, Larry Zbyszko, was sensational and that he should consider booking Larry into New York. And when McMahon saw Larry, he agreed right away. He also thought Larry was a terrific new talent.

Even while we watched Larry in action, McMahon was working on the angles. He said that when Zbyszko hit New York, they'd introduce him as Bruno Sammartino's prodigy. Vince thought that people would sit up and take notice of a guy who had trained with Bruno.

When I spoke to Larry about the plans, I explained to him that he'd be starting at the bottom of the ladder but it was a ladder that went from the basement of the Big Time all the way up to the Penthouse. I told him that the best way to climb that ladder was slowly and with with patience. I told him that in time I was sure he could be a tremendous headliner.

As the weeks rolled on, I didn't hear from Larry as often as I used to. At first, I didn't pay too much attention to this since I was immersed in my own affairs. Then some friends told me that Larry was having some serious personal problems.

Larry was reeling from the fallout of a failed marriage, one in which he had fathered a child. I also heard that he was very dissatisfied with the way he was moving up through the ranks of professional wrestling.

In early 1980, right at the time when he faced all this turmoil in his life, Larry approached me and said, "Look, Bruno...I'm going to be straight with you. I want you and me to put on an exhibition for television. I'm not talking about a regular match. I'm saying just for us to work out in the ring for the fans. What I want to do is show the fans just what caliber of wrestler I am because, let's face it, as long as I keep getting introduced as Bruno's prodigy, people will always look at me as some kind of rookie."

I disagreed with him and I told him so. "Larry, you're still a young guy who hasn't been at this game very long. It takes time to establish yourself. Right now, I think you're doing great. You're getting the right kind of matches, the right kind of publicity and you're climbing that ladder. In a couple of years, you're going to be a star and I think..."

He interrupted me right there. "A couple of years is too long to wait. I want to take you on right now...not a match...just a workout. That's all I'm asking."

I turned him down. I just didn't think it was a good idea for him at this stage of his career.

Without my knowledge or consent, Larry went to Vince McMahon and discussed the idea...and he got McMahon to side with him. McMahon thought it might really interest the fans. Nothing like it had ever been done before...just a strenuous workout between two pros. But even with Vince's support, the idea still didn't appeal to me.

Then Zbyszko did a television interview in which he announced his desire to stage a workout with his mentor, Bruno Sammartino. He said "I want to show you fans how my skills have developed but you might never get to see this. And do you know why? It's because Bruno has turned me down flat. He refuses to workout with me so I'd like to ask you, the public, how you feel about that. I'd like you to write or call me, Larry Zbyszko. Let me know."

And boy did the fans respond. Larry got a ton of mail urging Bruno to change his mind and hold that workout with him. They were saying, "Let the youngster show what he's learned.,,

At first, I didn't respond to this barrage of letters. I held back my comments and actually, I felt somewhat betrayed because I felt that it really was unnecessary for Zbyszko to go to the public and air something like this. As for McMahon, I'm sure he saw the workout as a way to generate income for himself.

Finally, after all the pressure from the fans, I agreed to the workout. I've always said that I'd do what the fans wanted me to do, whether it was to wrestle a certain opponent or appear in some exhibition. If the fans really wanted it, I would do it.

In March, 1980 Larry and I went at it. The rules were simple. We would to go into the ring only with the intention of trying to outmaneuver each other. If one of us showed that we were capable of putting a submission hold on the other, then the submission would be acknowledged and the hold would be released.

I said to Larry just before we were about to go on, "I know you think that I'm not the wrestler I was a few years ago...but I've been at this a long time and I have a lot of pride in what I can do. I'm not going to lay down for you. I'm in this all the way and I'm going to go all out."

Larry shrugged, "That's exactly what I want you to do."

Representatives from the State Athletic Commission conducted the official weigh-in. Then we climbed through the ropes and after a few preliminary announcements, the workout was on. As the 'match' proceeded, it was clear that I was outmaneuvering Larry. I'd apply holds and then release. But whenever Larry would lock me up with a hold, I had to break away because he would not release. He started getting frustrated early. I guess he thought that since I was such an older fellow, I would be falling over my own feet, back-pedaling to get away from him. He didn't expect me to be as quick and agile as I was.

During the workout, I called out to him a couple of times, suggesting that we just knock off. I could see he was was getting even more angry and frustrated. Finally, Zbyszko lost all his poise and a very ugly incident occurred. Larry had me in a hammerlock close to the ropes. I faked him one way then moved in another direction. He lost his balance and the momentum of my move caused me to bump him right through the ropes and out of the ring. As he climbed back in, I held the ropes for him to enter and whispered, "Larry, enough's enough. Let's call it a night."

Before I knew what happened, he drove a knee into my solar plexis and I was dead. The blow took the wind right out of me. I dropped to my knees and gasped desperately for air. I was absolutely knocked out. He had leveled me with a totally unexpected shot.

While I was down, Zbyszko scrambled over and grabbed a chair from just outside the ring. He charged at me, slamming the chair right onto my skull. A piece of metal ripped away a big chunk of skin over my eye. Blood from this wound began to cascade down my face. The exhibition was stopped at this point and I was rushed to a nearby hospital to get stitched back together again.

That of course was how the Sammartino/Zbyszko feud got started. I was very angry over what Zbyszko had pulled. Very upset. Naturally, McMahon and the other promotors saw it as a great story.

Reporters interviewed me a few days later and really rubbed it in, saying,

"We talked to Zbyszko and he say he wants to wrestle you for real. He claims he can beat you with one hand tied behind his back. What do you say to that, Bruno, especially after your prodigy put you out of commission in that workout." What did I say to that? Well, I wrestled him a number of times and we had some great matches.

Leaving the cage triumphant over Larry Zbyszko.

In August of 1980, Sammartino and Zbyszko drew 46,000 people to Shea Stadium. We pulled in over $550,000 in receipts and broke the all-time box office record for a wrestling show.

What made those figures all the more amazing was that on the same night, the Pittsburgh Steelers played an exhibition game against the New York Giants at Giant stadium, drawing 40,000 football fans. And the New York Yankees were taking on the Baltimore Orioles at Yankee Stadium, hosting 40,000 baseball fans. For wrestling to outdraw both football and baseball in the New York Metro area was a major accomplishment.

Some time later, I met Zbyszko in a cage match and I beat him handily. But I guess you just can't underestimate the nerve of some guys. After I retired that next year, even though I beat him a number of times, Zbyszko kept claiming, kept bragging that he was the one who retired Bruno Sammartino.

Of course, that's absolutely not true. As I've said before, I had been planning my retirement from wrestling for some time. It was something that I'd been promising my family as far back as 1977.

Before I did though, I had one more promise to keep. I had told Vince McMahon that I'd wrestle on the opening card at the new Meadowlands in New Jersey. The only problem was that due to delays in construction, the stadium wasn't going to be ready for us to use until October 4th, 1981.

While we waited for the workmen to finish, I made my official announcement to the world. The Meadowlands match would be my last appearance because I would be officially retiring. As it turned out, Japanese promoters contacted me when they heard about my plans and asked me to make a farewell tour of Japan. I had many great memories and had made many friends on previous trips there so I quickly agreed to one more swing through Japan.

Finally, October 4th rolled around. I went up against an opponent I knew well...George Steele. I handled George easily and won the match in about fifteen minutes. Then I took the microphone and thanked the fans for their wonderful support for so many, many years. I told them how much I had enjoyed wrestling for them and how I was going to miss them all. And then I made my exit. Unbelievable, but it was over...at least in the States.

Next day I caught a plane at Kennedy Airport and flew to Tokyo, a flight of nearly seventeen hours. Over a ten day period, I toured all the major Japanese cities that I had visited so many times before. In each city where I wrestled, an interpreter would tell the crowds for me that this would be the last time I would ever be in this particular city. I would tell them that I was retiring and how much I had enjoyed working in Japan.

FAREWELL TO BRUNO

FINAL WRESTLING MATCH
OF THE LIVING LEGEND
BRUNO SAMMARTINO

TONIGHT IN THE
BRENDAN BYRNE
MEADOWLANDS
ARENA

OFFICIAL SOUVENIR PROGRAM
SUNDAY, OCTOBER 4th, 1981

139

ベースボール・マガジン

プロレス & ボクシング

WRESTLING & BOXING

1

ブルーノ・サンマルチノVSジャイアント馬場

テリー・ファンク(左)
ドリー・ファンク・ジュニア

大場政夫

◆三大タイトル・マッチ完全詳報◆
剣ヶ峰をよく踏みこたえた馬場、猪木ら
◆特別読物◆
NWA王座をめぐる
ジュニアとモラレスの激しい対立
◆追跡レポート◆
"敵地"での砂糖水は苦すぎたサラバリア

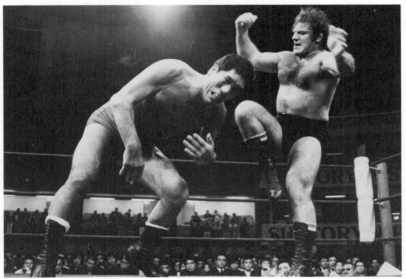

Highlights from one of my tours of Japan.

When I flew back home to Pittsburgh on October 15th. 1981, I was officially retired.

LIFE AFTER WRESTLING

When our first-born David was about five years old, I remember asking him, "David, what are you going to be when you grow up?"

Without hesitation David said, "I want to be a wrestler." We all laughed because we thought it was natural for a kid to want to be just what his Daddy

From a very early age, David wanted to be a wrestler.

143

is. When David reached the age of ten, we'd ask the same question and still get the same answer, "A wrestler." And when he got to be twelve, he'd say, "A professional wrestler." To tell you the truth, I started getting worried. I didn't want him to be involved with the business in any way, shape or form. I know that people will tell you that parents shouldn't interfere with their children's interests, but I had the experience to know what professional wrestling was all about.

Don't get me wrong! I'm very grateful for what wrestling has done for me. Because of the opportunities that grew out of circumstances as a child in Italy, what I'd built for myself in America was fantastic.

However, there were problems all along the way that were not so pleasant. I've told you about being on the road all the time, the serious injuries, not seeing my family for weeks. I've always admitted to myself that these aspects of the business did have significant downsides. Believe me, it has been an extremely difficult lifestyle at times.

I thought that if David followed through with the dream that he had since he was five years old, undoubtedly he would have to go through a lot of the same miseries that I went through. Naturally, as loving parents, Carol and I wanted all our sons to have the best chance for success in their own lives that they could possibly achieve and certainly better than what I had gone through. Because of wrestling's rewards, I could now offer my children an education and that was really the gift that I wanted to give them.

Early on, I started to get very concerned with David's constant talk about wrestling. Actually, he began wrestling in grade school and continued into Junior High. At that point, Carol and I thought that maybe if David went to a private school, perhaps he could be steered more toward academics. We had to face facts. Because of his passion for wrestling, his grades were not very high.

As he reached High School age, we took David to a school near Pittsburgh...Kiski High. This was a place that we felt would provide him with a solid foundation in scholastics. My old friend, Bill Cardille, the television announcer for the old Channel Eleven Studio Wrestling shows, had told me that his son was attending Kiski High. Both Bill and his son spoke very highly of the school.

After our visit to Kiski and taking some time to think about it, David consented, saying that he would like to go to the school. We were thrilled with his decision.

Since he hadn't done all that well with his grades in Junior High, he had to attend summer classes prior to his acceptance and bring his grades up to Kiski standards. This in itself was a good test for our son.

144

David and I in the backyard of our home.

*The Sammartino version of
"My Three Sons."*

145

And David did well that summer. He really is the kind of guy who succeeds if he puts his mind to it. His grades ended up earning him a place at Kiski High.

Once he was enrolled, David immediately joined the wrestling team at Kiski and bingo, the grades started sliding down again. After two years at Kiski, just as David should have been promoted to a Junior, we were advised that he would not be asked back for his last two years of High School. For the remainder of his schooling, David went back to public education at North Hills High School.

There he continued to train hard, working out with the weights and learning as much about wrestling as he could. He grew to be a very powerful young man. And no matter what I did to try to discourage him from wrestling, it was futile. He told us after graduation that he did not want to go on to college.

That's when I refused to continue helping him train. Both his Mother and I were very disappointed in this decision. My refusal to coach him made no difference to David. He found other coaches to help him hone his skills.

Then when David reached the age of nineteen, he announced to us the following "Mom, Dad...I've been working out for a long time and now I think I'm ready to take my shot. I'm going to work for a local promoter down in Texas that I've gotten hooked up with. He's willing to let me wrestle for him down there."

What could we do? Nothing. David was a very determined young man. He left home and went to the Lone Star State to wrestle professionally.

When we'd talk to him on the phone, it always seemed like the wrestling wasn't going very well. I would shrug my shoulders and say to my wife, "Maybe that's okay. He's still young. If things continue the way they're going, maybe he'll say the heck with this and come back and go to college."

Then the promoters sent me down to Texas for a couple of matches, which gave me an opportunity to see him work. He said his promoters had suggested it to him, so I agreed...not for the promoters' sake but just to see David.

The scenario was all too familiar to me. The wrestlers traveled by car three or four hundred miles each way...going from places like Amarillo to places like Lubbock. They'd put on their show then jump in the car and travel another four hundred miles.

And what do you know...the money that they were paying David wasn't enough for him to stay in any place other than a cheap little room. Since he couldn't afford restaurants, he would go to the local grocery in whatever town they stayed for the night, buy bread and ham, a gallon of milk and

146

go to his room to eat.

That kind of life was quite different than the one David knew growing

David strikes a pose.

up in our home, but it certainly was very familiar to me. Too familiar. In fact, it crushed me to see him going through it.

A long time ago I had made a promise to myself. After what I had experienced during the war and then coming to America, after the rough tough days of my early wrestling career, I said I never want to see any member of my family go through hardships like that. Never.

Yet here was my own son, right in front of my eyes, enduring the same stuff. I wasn't comparing what he was going through to what I had lived...at least not blow by blow, but here it was. The life I had tried to give him at home had turned into a cheap little hotel room where you ate ham sandwiches on the bed.

I tried to talk to him. I said, "David, now that you're getting a taste of what pro wrestling is like, how do you feel? Do you really want to put up with this nonsense? Why not come home and go back to school? Later if you still want to become a professional wrestler, then try again. I just think it's very important that you get that degree."

He fired right back at me, "Dad, of course I don't like what's happening. I don't like these long trips and I hate having to eat in my room, but I love wrestling. It's going to be my life and that's it! Okay?"

That trip to Texas showed me that no matter how difficult his situation might be, he was not going to be discouraged. Wrestling was in his blood, the way it has been in mine and nothing was going to make him quit.

Eventually, he moved from Texas to Puerto Rico where he wrestled for about six months, then he came back to the States. These days he's still in the game but I think he is finally getting a little disillusioned about it all. Right now, he's not with any big promoters and has been more or less wrestling for the Independents.

In fact, David's been to Japan and goes there two or three times a year. He still dreams, hopes that someday he'll be a headliner. I personally think he's very talented and he's got a tremendous physique on him. He's quick, strong and has a lot of wrestling savvy. David still wants to prove to himself and to everybody in the wrestling world that he can become a top attraction...if given the opportunity, maybe even a champion. Only time will tell.

When my twin boys, Danny and Darryl, were born in January of 1968, I had promised myself that I was going to spend more time at home with them than I had with David. It wasn't until I lost the title in 1971, that I truly started slowing down. By taking only matches here and there, I was able to be at home much more, changing diapers, feeding the babies, helping my wife and just being around the house as much as possible. That's what I really liked.

148

David at during one of his recent matches.

149

My wife was very happy when I was at home. You know, I had been on the road for so many years that it was almost like starting all over again. I started to feel like I was a part of my own family again.

Carol and I enjoy time together at home.

As the twins grew, they both became little leaguers. I used to get the biggest kick out of watching them play baseball. Both Danny and Darryl were pitchers. Both were very good and both developed elbow problems. Darryl's was especially bad. His coaches had seen that he had a strong arm for such a young kid and they started to teach him how to throw curve balls. He was fine for a couple of years then all of a sudden, Darryl started to have pain in his pitching arm.

I took him to the hospital to see Doc Steele, the Pirate physician. Doc Steele examined him and said within a couple of minutes, "Did they teach you how to throw curve balls?"

Darryl nodded and the Doc frowned, "That's what I was afraid of"

He explained to us how extensive the damage can be to a youngster who's encouraged to perform at levels that are way beyond the child's physical limitations. What happens is that calcium deposits form as the result of the pitching action and these deposits interfere with the normal growth of bone and tissue. The Doc ordered Darryl to quit pitching for a full year in the hopes that the problem would correct itself. After the year layoff, Darryl picked up the horsehide and tried to regain his pitching form, but it was

The twins turn four.

What a tag team!

Both Danny and Darryl loved sports.

151

no use. The damage had been done. The pain came back and he had to give up baseball. This was a big blow for the young guy because even at an early age, Darryl had aspirations to become a professional baseball player.

Danny, on the other hand, had little or no interest in baseball. He had abandoned that gentleman's game in High School for track events like throwing the shot and hurling the javelin.

Then a funny thing happened. Darryl, now out of baseball, showed up one day at Danny's track practice. He picked up his brother's javelin and tossed it a couple of times. Darryl quickly learned that the motion required for throwing the javelin was completely different than what was needed to throw a baseball. Throwing the javelin didn't hurt his elbow at all. He also discovered that he was pretty darn good at it besides.

Darryl joined the track team at North Hills High School, threw the javelin and very quickly broke the school record for that event...a mark that had stood for quite a few years. Also, in his first year on the team Darryl went to the State Finals. Later during his first year at Slippery Rock College, he made it to the National Finals in javelin, then had a return showing to the Nationals the next year. Not bad for an ex-pitcher.

Danny and Darryl pose with their grandmothers.

152

As it so happened, Danny had to quit throwing the javelin because...you guessed it...it bothered his arm. However, Danny went into weightlifting and at the age of twenty, was bench-pressing over 400 pounds. He continues to train to this day and is now 215 pounds of big husky young man.

I am also extremely proud to report that David, Danny and Darryl are clean from steroids. I've always been straight with them about drugs and the terrible dangers that are involved with their use. All of my sons have trained the honest way...with sweat and hard work.

Yes, it is so very true that I'm proud of my boys. I've really had a great time watching the twins grow up...something that I missed with David. I know that being with the twins helped me learn a lot about myself and I think it was good for them to have Dad around.

Danny and Darryl today.

Unfortunately with David, because I was on the road so much and because he was an only child until he was nearly eight, my oldest son experienced

153

a lot of tough times in school. When he was very small, he told me kids would pick on him, saying, "Oh, so your Dad's a wrestler, is he? Well, just how tough are you, shrimp?"

David would push right back, but as is the way with bullies, there would be more than one kid on him at a time and they would be bigger, older kids than he was. With regularity, David dragged himself home, sporting a bloody nose.

On the other hand, the twins were always together, protecting each other. As a result, neither one went through the bullies' rituals as David did.

In 1981, when I flew back from Japan, now officially retired, one fortunate thing was that I still had both of my parents around. Throughout my career, particularly in the later years, as I traveled around the world, I began to worry more and more about my parents. I always had this nagging fear that something might happen while I was in Korea or Japan, Australia or Singapore, and no one in the family would be able to reach me.

The years were piling up for them. My Dad was born on February 7, 1891 and my Mom was born on August 3, 1898. By the time October, 1981 rolled around, Dad was approaching his 91st year and my Mom had just celebrated her 83rd birthday. After I retired, I was so grateful that I could spend time with both of them then.

Dad's age was beginning to catch up with him.

154

Unhappily, my Dad's health had begun to fail him as he moved into his tenth decade. Since Mom was in her 80's, it was becoming increasingly difficult for her to do all the things she had been accustomed to do and to help Dad besides.

Well, if there's one thing you can say about the Sammartino family, it is that we are close-knit. Because we are so close, none of us wanted to hear one minute about the possibility of putting Dad into a nursing home. I'm not saying that there's anything wrong with doing something like that, but for us that wasn't a solution. My Mom sure didn't want any part of it and I know it would have been the end of Dad had he been put out to pasture in one of those places.

My sister Mary, without question one of the greatest persons I've known in my life, was ready to volunteer to quit her job at the bank in order to help out at our parents' home. I told Mary not to worry. I said, "Look, you should keep your job. I've got plenty of time now that I can spend with Mom and Dad. Let me help out."

And that's what we did. Every day, I'd get up early and do my road work. Even though retired, I was still dedicated to physical fitness. After finishing my training for the morning, I'd drive over to Mom and Dad's and be there around 9:30 a.m., about the time Dad usually got up. Mom would have the coffee already brewing and would follow along behind Dad as he made his way to the breakfast table.

Even at his advanced age, there were certain things that Dad refused to let me help him with. For instance, although it might sound funny, he would only let Mom dress and undress him. At her age that was difficult for her, but she was willing to do it for Dad.

Throughout his life, Dad had been a strong, proud man. He spent some nine years fighting for Italy in the calvary and had been decorated twice for his service during World War I. After the war, he worked as a blacksmith in the Old Country. Later, he traveled to America, working hard in the mines, in construction and even used his blacksmith skills repairing tools for a time. Then, for the latter part of his working career, he labored in the steel mills, quitting only when he was forced to retire in his early seventies.

He always was a robust and rugged person. His tremendous pride in his own abilities made it tough for him to face the final years of his life when he needed so much help.

I would always be there every single morning, urging him to use his walker. The doctor had said that if he didn't exercise every day, he might reach the point where he couldn't move at all. So I'd say, "Come on, Pop. We have to walk now."

155

And we'd walk all around their house. Sometimes we'd make it to the front porch where we'd sit for a while. Then I'd stay with him and my Mom until they ate their main meal which would be around 2:00 in the afternoon. We Italians always like to eat this meal early in the day.

After dinner, my parents would take their naps. I would help Dad down into his favorite sofa chair. By the time their nap was over, Mary would be home from work and she would look in on them.

We have always been a very close family. That's my brother Paul on my right and my sister Mary holding my hand. Mom and Pop are in front.

Although saddened as I was to witness my Dad's deteriorating condition, I was thankful that I could be there for him now in my own retirement. I hoped that it made up a little for all those years that I was on the road and couldn't be with him and my Mom.

During this time, I enjoyed many private moments with my Dad. I could still talk with him, sitting and reminiscing about the Old Country. As the months wore on, he started slipping and I noticed that he wouldn't be able to remember certain people or events. Despite that, Dad always knew who was with him in his own house. He never lost complete control by any means although eventually he did begin to have flights of fancy.

156

For almost four years, I was there with Dad every day and although we went through the same routine daily, I was so very very happy to have had that time with him.

Sadly, my Dad passed away in 1985, at the age of 94. I remember some people said to me, "Well, he lived a long life and 94 years is a long, long time for someone to be around."

That sort of comforting always bothered me although I understand that those people meant well. When you love your parents or when you love anybody and they die, it doesn't ease the pain you feel at their passing to be told that they lived such a long, long life. Whether they were 50 or 70 or 90, does your love for this person diminish because of their age? Not for me.

We buried our beloved father and my Mother's husband. Now my brother and sister and I spent as much time as we could with Mom.

THE WINDS OF CHANGE

Back in 1981, I had just returned home from a Far East tour to hear the news that Vince McMahon had gone into a Florida hospital. Right away, I called his home down there and talked to his wife, Juanita, who didn't volunteer much information about Vince's condition. Instead, she gave me the hospital number and suggested I call her husband myself.

I phoned Vince immediately and asked him what was going on. He joked a little bit and said that it wasn't pretty. Vince told me that he was passing blood in his urine. He said one of the doctors had told him that he had a bladder tumor and that they had to operate as soon as possible.

That's what they did. The surgeon removed what they could of the tumor and then after he sewed Vince back up, warned him that a second operation would probably be necessary sometime down the road. Well, his wife didn't like that diagnosis and wanted Vince to get another opinion.

When McMahon got his second opinion, this doctor drew him a completely different picture. The second doctor said that the first doctor was all wet and that Vince didn't need follow up surgery. As a matter of fact, Doctor #2 merely prescribed medication and told Vince that if he simply took this medication, then he'd be fine in no time.

When Vince heard this news, he got very angry with Doctor #1 and religiously followed Doctor #2's advice up until the time he died in 1984. It's true that Vince took the medication and was okay for quite some time...nearly two and a half years. But in early 1984, Vince started to pass blood again. He ignored it for a while, then when he reported it to Doctor #2, he was put on yet another kind of medication. By the time everybody figured out that the medications weren't doing the job, it was too late.

When they finally got Vince back in the hospital, they found out that Doctor #1 had been right all along. The bladder tumor had come back and had spread throughout his entire body. And that's what killed him. He died in May of 1984.

After Vince passed on, his son Vince McMahon, Jr. came charging to the fore and took over his late father's wrestling business. Actually, Vince, Jr. had been running the show for quite some time while his father had been getting progressively worse.

Toward the middle of that summer, Vince, Jr. called me and posed a question to me. How would I like to come back to wrestling as a television color commentator? That's exactly what I'd done for his father back in 1978 and I had really enjoyed it at the time. His offer caught my interest

158

interest.

In my dressing room with Vince McMahon, Sr.

Then Vince, Jr. added the kicker. He said that he would be willing to give my son, David, a break and bring him into the WWF. That would mark a real beginning for David because even though he'd been at it for several years, he still wasn't wrestling for any big organization.

I considered the arrangement and said yes to it. First, it would be an important step forward for David to hook up with Vince, Jr. and second, I could sit back and comment on the action instead of being right in the middle of it. The other added benefit was that the shows were taped only every three weeks so I wouldn't have to hit the road that often. It sounded great.

After David started with the WWF and I had begun my commentator's role, McMahon approached David with an idea. He said, "Your dad is still in better shape than most of the guys out there today. He's still lifting. He's running seven and eight miles every day. Even though his weight's down, he could put back ten pounds and not be flabby. What I'm saying is why don't you and he team up for tag team matches? It'd be one of a kind. You know, father and son."

Well, even though I wasn't thrilled with the idea I didn't want to be the reason for David not getting ahead in professional wrestling, so I accepted his idea. In March, 1985, David and I joined up as a tag team for the first time. We wrestled together in Philadelphia and the place sold out. I remember getting goose bumps from the crowd's cheers. Though I hadn't been there in four years, the fans gave me a standing ovation when we entered. It was something that touched me...and energized me.

When I went into the ring, I wanted to be the Bruno Sammartino that everyone remembered. Of course, I'm not going to claim that suddenly I was transformed into the old Bruno, but I went in there with my old spirit and did the best I could under the circumstances. It turned out to be a good match and David did very well for himself.

David and I played Philadelphia a couple more times and we worked Pittsburgh, New York and Boston that year. After that short swing through those cities, I decided again that I had had enough and took off the tights once more.

Well, when I did this, David had a peculiar reaction. He started to act out, saying that now he felt he had been used. He said to me, "Dad, you know it's true. The only time I'm a headliner is when I wrestle with you. With the tag team dissolved, I'm just back to being a preliminary boy. It's making me mad."

David got depressed about all this and began to behave quite unreasonably. He got to be very confused about it all. One day he would quit wrestling and the next day he would want to come back. He told me once, "I know what my role is here. The promoters just want me around so that anytime they want you to put the tights back on, they call me. But really they just use me to get you back into the ring. Then when the match is over, I stop being Bruno's son. I'm back to being David Nobody when we aren't wrestling together."

I tried to tell him that because the game had changed since my day, we had to face facts. "Look, David, the WWF is now the only act in town. In my day, the country was divided up into territories and different promoters had the Northeast, the Midwest, the South, the North. Now Vince, Jr. holds the keys to success. You have to play ball with him or you're out."

Ever since the death of his father, McMahon, Jr. had become a very aggressive promoter. He had expanded to the point where he was gobbling up everybody's territory all across the country. If you wanted to wrestle in the big leagues, you had to deal with Vince, Jr.

David's other option was the National Wrestling Alliance, still active but certainly not as big as the WWF. Frankly, I don't think the NWA really considered putting David on their roster simply because I was still with the WWF.

When McMahon, Jr. asked me to start accepting matches yet another time, I found myself in a strange position. Even though I despised the circumstances, I felt I had to go along with Vince, Jr. for David's sake. If I cooperated with him and then if David wanted to come back professionally, I would be able to say to Vince, Jr., "I realize that David's made a few mistakes in judgement. He'd like to make amends and give it another shot. How about another chance for him?"

I reasoned that McMahon, Jr. would take David back into the fold because certainly if he expected me to go along with his requests, then Vince, Jr. would have to respect my wishes. We played this tune several times. And each time, David would climb back in the ring, wrestle for a while, get extremely frustrated for the same catalog of reasons and then would quit again. It wasn't a real comfortable situation for anyone.

Another reason that I hated getting back in the ring was what I perceived was happening with professional wrestling. I just did not like what I was seeing in the sport as the 80's wore on. Professional wrestling was changing in a drastic and for me unacceptable way. Wrestling no longer resembled anything I had known and the changes weren't for the good, believe me.

I despised what Vince McMahon, Jr. had done to professional wrestling. It had become a complete, total cartoon. Even though gimmicks existed in my day and there were things that I fought promoters about back then, I never thought that the game would become as bizarre as it had gotten by the end of the 1980's. Finally, I wanted nothing to do with it.

Wrestling was taking its toll.

There was a whole list of incidents that turned my stomach. For example, in 1985 I did a Piper's Pit interview in Madison Square Garden with this guy Roddy Piper. Typical of what was going on in wrestling, he started to say extremely derogatory remarks about me. Then he escalated even those tasteless rantings and went on to insult my heritage. He did so in a manner that was strong even for this day and age. It reminded me of the insults we had to endure from school children when we first came to the United States. His insults and baiting led to a number of fast and furious matches between myself and Piper.

I even wrestled for a while as a substitute. McMahon, Jr. would pull me in at the last minute to sub for guys who were either hurt or couldn't pass their drug test.

Of course, I felt abused. Here I was, Bruno Sammartino, the man known for twenty years as the Living Legend, the man who sold out arena after arena and now I was reduced to filling in for kids who suffered injuries because they weren't in shape or replacing youngsters who couldn't stay off drugs long enough to earn a living in what was a sport filled with tremendous opportunities. All this really affected me deep in my guts.

Finally, I leveled with David. I told him, "Son, it doesn't make any sense for me to wrestle anymore. You're going to have to make or break it on your own without me there to twist Vince, Jr.'s arm for you. Either accept things the way they are or quit and find some other way to make a living."

After that one last talk, David tried one more come back. But when he found out that the WWF intended to keep booking him into the smallest arenas, that was enough for him...again. Once more he left the WWF totally disillusioned.

Where that left me was clear. Now I wanted no part of climbing through the ropes and into the ring again. I decided to tell Vince, Jr. that I was out for good.

I tried to contact McMahon, Jr. three or four times but he never returned any of my calls. I wanted to let him know that I had an offer outside of his organization and that I wanted to take it. Finally, in an effort to contact him indirectly, I spoke with a fellow who worked under Vince, Jr. and explained to this person what was on my mind and why I wanted to speak with McMahon, Jr. Although I still heard nothing directly from the young promoter, I found out that he apparently had gotten the word.

It was McMahon Jr.'s wife, Linda, who called and asked me why I had been calling.

I told her I had a job offer elsewhere which was much more attractive than staying with the WWF. Well, Linda jumped in and started to browbeat me about where she felt I stood with them. She told me that the WWF had some basic rights concerning what I did and how I used my own name and that I had better watch my step.

Before she got too far into her tirade, I stopped her. I said, "Let me give you a little history lesson, Linda. I feel that I am probably more responsible for the success that the WWF has experienced than anyone else. Back when your business was known as the WWWF, it wasn't much of anything. It struggled and your late father-in-law really came close to folding many times."

"It was only after I took the title that the organization rose to the top. Bruno Sammartino as champion drew the crowds.

Linda tried to interrupt me, but I wouldn't let her. I kept laying into her. "Here's another thing for you to look at. When I lost the title in 1971, having held it for nearly eight years, the WWF's gate attendance fell again. I wasn't wrestling as much as I had after I lost the title and Vince, Sr., asked me to come back and wrestle as much as could to help bail them out. I tell you, Linda, I remember one time that Vince, Sr. and your husband met me at the airport and padded along behind me like puppies, begging me to return to the fold."

Linda finally burst in, talking over what I was saying. She told me that the reason I could land jobs elsewhere was because of what the WWF had done for *me* over the years.

With that I grew frustrated and said goodbye to her. I resented her remarks very, very much. Of course, I guess I shouldn't have been surprised by anything that bunch would say or do. The kind of people that they are will stop at nothing to advance themselves.

So I left wrestling and I left it for good. Doing this made me feel as if somebody had lifted a thousand pound weight off my back. During those years when I had ventured back into the ring chiefly for my son's benefit, the whole circus atmosphere professional wrestling had assumed completely embarrassed me. I felt terrible that I was still involved with it on any level.

Since the final split, I've been asked many times if I would ever consider getting back into wrestling. I've always maintained that if a league evolved that was interested in reviving the legitimate kind of wrestling, then I would consider it.

LOOKING BACK

I guess when you've been in one business for a long time you're bound to get philosophical when you finally leave that enterprise. I'm no exception.

I'll always think back on professional wrestling with memories of both the good and the bad. That's just the way life is. Nothing's perfect...one way or the other. Sometimes you get the bear and sometimes the bear gets you. Then sometimes the bear turns out to be a skunk in a bearskin rug.

One issue that really bothered me throughout my career was what newspaper writers would say about wrestling. The ink never varied, be it in Pittsburgh, New York, Boston or San Francisco. The sports scribes would tell their readers that all wrestling matches are rehearsed. They'd write that wrestlers spend the time before their bouts in the dressing rooms, practicing what moves they're going to use on each other.

If those wordsmiths had ever been backstage and had seen this preparation going on for themselves that would be a different thing. I'd shrug and say, "Well, guys looks like I've been wrong all these years. Even though I've never rehearsed a match in my life, I guess everybody else was doing it and I never noticed. You saw it with your own eyes so I suppose you have every right to report the story."

Of course, the reports were ridiculous. Let me give you some details of the backstage mechanics that are involved in a wrestling exhibition. Let's take the Civic Arena in Pittsburgh, for example. In this facility, you have one dugout where all of the wrestlers emerge from their dressing rooms. That doesn't mean that the wrestlers are all waiting in one large room. The dugout contains a dozen of these dressing rooms and opponents are never assigned to the same room. That means you don't come face to face with the man you're wrestling until the moment you get into the ring. Another example would be Madison Square Garden. There the dressing rooms are far removed from one another.

And besides, how could rehearsals for a match take place amidst the State Athletic Commission members, the referees, the doctors, the time-keepers? You see, it's not just the wrestlers back there. It's everybody that's involved with the program. So where would you rehearse for a match?

A second question might be "When do you rehearse all the moves that might come up in a match?" Think about it. Many of my matches went sixty minutes or longer. In fact, I've had matches that have lasted an hour and forty-five minutes. And you're wrestling practically every day. So when would you have the time to rehearse all these moves?

Third question..."How do you rehearse these moves?" How can you practice going over the top rope in the dressing room? How can you try out body slams or drop kicks in the dressing room?

Of course, anyone with any common sense, which excludes a lot of sports writers, would realize that it's absolutely bizarre to think that anything so complicated could be prearranged. We'd have to be a bunch of Einsteins to learn these routines, not only on any given night but on every single night of the week.

Just think when a broadway play is put on, the actors rehearse their lines for months before they go on stage in front of an audience. My God, if what the writers say is true, then wrestlers are the greatest actors that the human race has ever known. Every night we rehearse the equivalent of a full-length production with different opponents in a different part of the country and then move on to a new presentation somewhere else the next day. Give me a break, Mister Media Writer.

Another issue that the media people brought up...and one that really bugged me too...is whether or not wrestlers use blood capsules. We've talked about that earlier, but let me just say a few more words about it.

I remember one time when I was wrestling Ivan Koloff, the man who would eventually take my first championship belt away from me in 1971. It was a typical Koloff match...tough, gutsy, full of action. Just after he came off the ropes one time, I dealt him a powerful blow and split him open right above the eye. Blood poured out of that wound.

Later when Doc Civitarese was sewing up Koloff's injury, one of the officials from the State Athletic Commission went up to a sports reporter from a Pittsburgh newspaper. The official asked the reporter if he would like to come back to the dressing room and see for himself how badly Koloff had been cut.

The reporter refused, yet the next day he wrote an article suggesting that Koloff had used chicken blood in a capsule to fake his injury. The reporter wrote this garbage after having refused to go and see for himself how severely Koloff had been hurt. He was one writer who always intended to spew out derogatory stories about wrestling. Naturally, he would refuse to go back to the dressing room. He would have seen the reality of the situation and that would have killed his nice, neat story.

All too often when media people were feeling feisty, when they wanted to puff themselves up by tearing others down, when they had nothing better to do than make up false stories, they would hike over to the wrestling arenas and proceed to rip apart the wrestlers by writing half-truths and innuendoes. Very seldom would they feature wrestlers who had gone to the Olympics as representatives of the United States. Hardly ever would they churn out a positive story about National AU champion wrestlers who were in our business. Nor would they say kind things about pros who had achieved greatness in other sports like weightlifting or football.

These dirty-collared columnists only wanted to write the bad rap, the mean-spirited angle, the sly lie. Many fans were insulted by this bilge simply because they were there and saw the matches and then after reading about it in the newspaper the next day, came away wondering, what in the world had the reporter seen? I do admit, however that there were fans who did believe the trash they read, because unfortunately some people believe anything.

I remember when I broke my neck in that match with Stan Hansen. A reporter made the suggestion that it was all hype, done to maximize the gate for a return bout. Okay, Mister Reporter...did you go to Doctor Civitarese or any of the other doctors who attended to me in the hospital? Did you hear what they had to say? Did you examine the X-Rays that were taken and determine that they were falsified?

Ridiculous. A hospital isn't going to involve itself in a conspiracy to increase box office revenues for the wrestling profession. But then again, why should reporters actually investigate their allegations? Why shouldn't they just write what they want to? After all, investigation might turn up the facts and that would ruin a good lie. Like they say, nothing spoils an exciting news story more than a good eyewitness.

167

Bring on your toughest opponent.

I believe that the promoter should bear a lot of the burden for the media's lack of respect for the wrestling profession. Ever since the gimmicks and the show business razzledazzle took over, our sport has suffered in the eyes of its critics.

The wrestlers are the ones who've paid for it all. On the one hand, we go into the ring and absorb the blows, suffer the injuries and at times, face their crippling consequences. Then after we endure the pains for the sport we love best, the media people tell the public that it's all make-believe.

To me, this has been the most frustrating aspect of my sports career. You train all your life to prepare for professional wrestling, then you go into the ring and give it everything you've got only to have some writer or sports analyst question your very integrity. It's heart-breaking.

Once I remember confronting one of my media critics and saying to him, "Look, my friend, since you suggest that I'm a no-talent fake...just an actor in trunks, then get me somebody you regard as a real athlete. Bring me a tough guy from any sport. I don't care who. Just bring this man around and then put him in the ring with me. Let's see what will happen."

Of course, my challenge was never met. Most athletes wouldn't dare to fool with a wrestler. The truth is most athletes fear and respect professional wrestlers. Maybe my challenge was foolish in and of itself, but sometimes out of pure frustration, you want to show these media assassins just where they're wrong.

Another aspect of professional wrestling that took its toll on all of us was and still is the loneliness of it all. Because wrestling is not a team sport like professional baseball or football, a wrestler often turns into a loner. That's just the facts of life. Wrestlers are always traveling to different arenas every day of the week. In fact in my era, you constantly wrestled for different promoters around the country and around the world.

One night, you might run into sixteen different guys at the Civic Arena. Then the next night, you're off in one direction and the sixteen other guys are off to Detroit or New York or Baltimore. That tends to make you into a loner real fast. You had your schedule and everybody else had theirs.

I really had very few close friends who came out of professional wrestling. One exception was Dominic Denucci. He was born and raised not too far from my home town in Italy. Believe it or not, we never met until we both were touring Australia in 1966. He's just a super guy, a great wrestler and we've remained good friends to this day. But aside from Dominic, there have been few others from the world of wrestling whom I would call a close friend.

I've talked a bit now about some of the more negative aspects of my career. Of course, there were many other experiences that I've had that pulled the balance way back into the positive. Actually, all through my stint as a professional wrestler, I've been like a small kid in many ways. No matter what fame I may have achieved, whenever I met top professional sports or show business figures I was always in awe.

One fellow whom I call truly a friend is Jilly Rizzo, who was Frank Sinatra's right hand man for many years. Jilly also owned one of the best nightclub/ restaurants in New York City. We got to be great friends and he was always very nice to me. In fact, Jilly introduced me to New York you might say, showing me where all the great restaurants were and who had the best entertainment...places like the Latin Quarter and the Copacabana.

Hobnobing with the late Liberace.

Basically, I was the kind of guy who wrestled, grabbed a bite to eat and went straight to bed because I wanted to get up early the next morning and go to the gym for my workout. But Jilly made me stray from that routine a few times. He would always come to the Garden to see me, then he'd invite me over to his establishment. That was where I got a chance to met a lot of celebrities who also enjoyed Jilly's company, his menu and his shows. I met people like Frank Sinatra, Sammy Davis, Jr., Peter Lawford, Richard Conte and even Liberace.

But of all the entertainers I ever met, I think the nicest, most down-to-earth guy was Jimmy Durante, whom I met in Philadelphia at a dinner to honor me for winning the championship. When Durante performed, we all fell in love with him...a true star.

Other names I could mention include Jimmy Rosselli, a man with a fantastic singing voice. Then there was Enzo Stuarte and Sergio Franchi. I don't want to forget comic Pat Cooper, otherwise known as Pasqualie Caputo, who I knew years before he became a headliner. But that's the way it was in my business. It gave me a chance to meet lots of people that I would never have had the chance to meet otherwise.

Now I'm going to let you in on a little secret. With most of these stars that I met, I was terribly disappointed. I didn't find them to be the genuine people that I had imagined them to be. Although they were usually nice to

170

The "Schnoz" was really down to earth.

me, I watched each one and saw what he or she did when a fan came around. I saw a lot of them quickly turn around and become very unfriendly to that fan, getting temperamental and putting on this great show of arrogance. After a while, I reached a point where I just didn't want to meet any more of these show business celebrities. Who needed their bad attitudes?

I've always admired people who have achieved greatness in whatever they've set out to do and then have remained "of the people". Those celebrities who put themselves above everyone else, like they're something special are the ones that I lose complete respect for.

As great a talent as Frank Sinatra might have been for so many, many years, I found him to be extremely temperamental. In fact, one time in Pittsburgh, Sinatra embarrassed me terribly.

It was in the late 1960's and Sinatra was scheduled to perform at the Civic Arena. Channel Eleven was the local television station that carried wrestling programs and the one that I had been closely involved with. One of Eleven's people who knew that I was an acquaintance of Sinatra's, asked me if I could arrange for an interview with him. And they asked me to do the interview.

Now I had been told that Sinatra wasn't very cooperative when it came to doing such things, but I went ahead and called Jilly Rizzo and asked Jilly if he could check it out for me. In a short while, Jilly called back, said Sinatra had been in a good mood and had agreed to the interview. Great so far.

When the day came we got a whole group together...the general manager of Channel Eleven and his wife...the program director and his wife...my good friend Bill Cardille and his wife...my family...some of my wife's family...and a priest who was a friend of mine, Father Gino Rivey. We gathered all these people together, adding the film crew and their truck.

We all went to the location where the interview had been slated and we were setting up for it when I saw Jilly walking toward me. He definitely had

172

an upset face on. I said, "Jilly, what's the matter? What's going on?"

Jilly shook his head. "Frank's in a bad mood."

I said, "Boy, I hope that doesn't mean he won't do this interview. I got everybody here for it...all the big shots from Channel Eleven...my family... Father Gino..."

When Jilly didn't say anything, I knew we were in trouble. Not only had Sinatra refused to do the interview, he wouldn't even come out of his room and speak with us.

I was incredibly embarrassed. I thought that if I tell all the people who are waiting to see Sinatra that he's in a bad mood now and won't budge from his suite that they'd consider me crazy for dragging them over there. Maybe they'd think I had just been trying to be a big shot.

Finally, I confronted everybody, apologized and said that the whole thing was off. Sinatra was in a bad mood and wouldn't see anyone right now. When my guests heard that, I was surprised at their reaction. Nobody got particularly upset although they were all disappointed. Most everyone said that big stars like that always have a bad temperament. Everybody understood and believed what I'd said.

As a matter of fact before this incident happened, I had often been invited to join Sinatra at his special table at Jilly's. This table was Sinatra's and nobody but nobody would sit there unless Frank was in town and he invited you to sit down. When I had joined him and his other guests on those occasions, I had often witnessed his outbursts of temper. That should have been my warning I suppose.

After that, I guess I don't have to tell you what my feelings were toward old Mr. Blue Eyes. Although I met him several more times, I chose not to be in his company for long. I decided I didn't want to be associated with people like that.

In contrast to all these celebrities, big shots, little shots and other self-important people that I've known, let me tell you about one little boy from Pittsburgh, whose name was Frankie, too.

In 1968, I got a telephone call from Channel Eleven sportscaster, Red Donnally. Red told me, "Bruno, I have a big favor to ask of you. There's a little boy, maybe ten or eleven at the most and he's very sick in the hospital...Allegheny General. He's a big fan of yours and if you could pay him a visit I'm sure it would really give him a lift."

I said sure. When I went to see little Frankie, that was his name as I found out, it really tore at me. He was so sick that I wasn't certain that he even knew I was there. I just sat at his bedside with his mother beside me and his father, standing on the opposite side of the bed near the window. With tears in her eyes, his mother told me, "Just talk to him, Bruno. He adores you and he can hear everything we say."

So I said to him, "Frankie, I hear you're a big wrestling fan. I'm so very happy to meet someone like you and I'd like to see you get better real soon. I want you to come to the Civic Arena as my guest and watch me wrestle, okay?"

When I saw tears in the eyes of little Frankie's Mom and Dad, I got choked up myself. What was really heartbreaking was what his Dad told me out in the hall as I was about to leave. He said that Frankie had leukemia.

After my visit, when I got home I called up Red Donnally and asked him to follow what happens with Frankie while I was out of town. I wanted to make good on my promise about taking him to the Civic Arena to watch me wrestle. I wanted to know if Frankie was going to bounce back.

In a few weeks, lo and behold, I got the wonderful news from Red that little Frankie had indeed made a comeback. He'd been given numerous blood transfusions along with other medical wonders. He had seemingly taken a few faltering steps back to health.

And you know, he had heard everything that I had told him during my visit. Now he excitedly told his Mom that he wanted to come to the Arena for the wrestling matches and especially to see Bruno.

I was so delighted to hear that Frankie had bounced back. I asked Red to find out just who Frankie wanted to bring with him. Once I knew that I would make all the arrangements.

I remember that that we had decided to meet backstage at the Arena before the matches began. When I came out of the dressing room area and saw Frankie with his two friends, his eyes just gleamed. I handed him his tickets and brought him in to meet some of the other wrestlers.

We spent a little time together just talking. I told Frankie to stay well and do everything the doctors wanted him to do and to listen to his Mom and Dad. Then the kids went inside to their front row seats and had a great time.

Later I discovered that Frankie's family was very, very poor. His parents were decent people who had a lot of bad luck and had ended up with nothing. How sad it was to know that the boy had so many needs, so many problems and everything couldn't be done that needed to be done for him.

Some months later, my wife Carol had to go into Allegheny General Hospital for disc surgery. Having been out of town on tour, I went straight to the hospital to visit my wife. All of a sudden, we heard a little commotion going on in the hallway outside of our room. It sounded like somebody was having an argument with a child.

I stepped out into the hallway to find little Frankie pleading his case to a nurse. A policeman stood by, ready to escort Frankie out of the building. His back was to me so he didn't see me right away. He said, "I have to get in and see Mrs. Sammartino. Bruno's my friend. They're both my friends."

I spoke up. "Frankie, what are you doing here?"

He spun around and was shocked to see me. "Bruno, I thought you'd be wrestling someplace. It's great to see you!"

"Frankie, why don't you wait right here and I'll straighten this whole thing out in a minute." Then I pulled the Nurse and the Police Officer aside, out of Frankie's earshot and told them all about Frankie, his illlness, his love for wrestling and what a big fan he was of me and my family. The two understood and said, "Okay."

I brought Frankie into my wife's room and announced, "Dear, here's a good friend of mine I want you to meet. His name is Frankie."

Frankie was so happy that he could visit with Carol. We sat and talked for ten minutes or so, the Frankie sneaked a look at my wrist watch. He stood up and said, "I guess I better get going. It's a long walk home."

Just for conversation I asked him how far away did he live from the hospital. He replied, "It's about an hour and a half walk."

I said, "My gosh, Frankie. You mean you walked an hour and a half to visit my wife?"

He nodded and probably wondered what the big deal was.

"Frankie, there's no way you're going to walk back." I pulled out my wallet and gave him fifteen dollars. "Here's what I want you to do, Frankie. I can't leave my wife right now to give you a ride. I want to spend some more time with her and then after my visit is over, I have to go straight from here to the airport. So you take this money..."

As I handed him the money, he looked like I was making a big mistake. He gulped and said, "Bruno, do you know how much money you're giving me?"

I said, "Frankie, it's all right. You take this money. I want you to buy a milkshake for yourself first. Then you jump on a bus for home and you can keep the change for whenever you have to visit someone else."

He couldn't believe his good fortune. Before he left, he paused in the doorway and gave us a big smile and wave. He was so happy at that moment.

A short time after Frankie visited Carol in the hospital, Frankie's parents sent me a short letter, telling me how grateful they were that I was Frankie's friend. They said that the friendship meant so much to him.

Later that month, I went on an overseas tour. I would think about little Frankie every so often. I made a promise to give him a call when I got back. After I returned to Pittsburgh, I got Frankie's number from Red

175

Donnally and telephoned to check up on him. Frankie's mother answered and when I told her who I was, she started crying on the phone. Through her tears, she told me that little Frankie had been buried five days earlier. The whole thing touched me so very deeply that I began crying, too. Frankie's death made me very, very sad for a long, long time.

So we can talk about big shots and we can talk about people who really mean something. There was another young man that I met who I can never forget. His name was Johnny and he lived in New York...but he spent most of his time in Roosevelt Hospital because he had cancer.

I remember that Johnny's mother called me up at the station where I was doing a live interview. She caught me just after we went off the air. She had a simple request. Could I please come and visit her son in the hospital. She told me all about Johnny's problem.

Of course I agreed.

When I arrived at the hospital and went to Johnny's room to visit him, I found out that the entire floor where he was staying was filled with cancer patients...and they were all children. Some of them looked healthy, ordinary kids, out in the hallways bouncing balls and playing.

Then I stepped into Johnny's room and he was in a plastic tent, laboring for every breath he took. When he caught sight of me, his spirits rose. Johnny was elated to have me as a visitor. I gave him some pictures and a magazine. He accepted them gratefully, not really believing I was there in the same room with him.

Before I left, I told him that on Saturday I was going to be on television wrestling and that when I was interviewed, I would look right at him and say Hi. He said he'd be watching.

To be honest, the way that poor Johnny looked under that plastic tent, I never could have believed he would be around on Saturday. I was visiting him on Wednesday. Saturday was almost four whole days away.

In the hallway, his mother spoke to me very quietly. She said, "Johnny's doctors have told us that he has very little time left. Thank you for telling him that you'll say hi to him on television but Saturday is a very long way away off for him."

Saturday rolled around and I told Ray Morgan, the host of the wrestling show and the guy who was going to interview me that I had a special request. During his questions, I wanted to have just ten seconds to say hello to a little boy in the hospital.

Ray said sure.

That Saturday evening, I went on the air and I interrupted Ray a few seconds into the interview and said to the camera, "I just want to say hello to a young man in Roosevelt Hospital who's a very dear friend of mine. Hello, Johnny. I want you to know that I'm thinking about you. I want you to take care of yourself and I'll see you real soon.''

I'm awaiting my interview during a live TV telecast.

About a week later, I was appearing in New Jersey. While I was in my dressing room, waiting for the call, two policeman came to the door and knocked. They told me that there was a couple down the hall who wanted to see me because I knew their son.

When I came out, I walked over to find Johnny's Mother and Father waiting for me. We shook hands and then before I could ask how Johnny was, his mother spoke.

She said, "After you left the hospital that day, Johnny was so very happy. But then he got real sick all the rest of that week. The doctors couldn't understand how he hung on. Finally, Saturday was here and Johnny waited all day for the wrestling show. When you came on and greeted him, he had such a wonderful smile on his face.''

177

With this, she stopped short, unable to speak any further. Johnny's father finished the story for her. He said, "Well, Bruno, Johnny died about thirty minutes after he saw you on TV. He stuck around just to see you."

I think by now with what I have told you about myself that you know me to be a man who can endure pain. You can break my arm and I will keep on going. Break my leg and I will withstand it. I broke my neck and I refused to take pain killers. I don't need those kinds of drugs because I can take the pain.

But when terrible things happen to folks like Johnny and little Frankie, I become the weakest man in the world. I can't control my tears and I feel like a weakling. This is what goes to the heart and stays there.This is what's real.

Big shots? Who are they? I hope I am never mistaken for one.

I remember once I received a request to go to the Veteran's Hospital in New Haven, Connecticut. The man who phoned me sounded like he was in a panic. He told me the date he had in mind and it was a day I couldn't do it. We talked a bit and agreed to shoot for the next day after that which was okay with him.

Then he asked me a strange question. "And what will your fee be, Bruno?"

I was surprised. "Don't be silly. Why would there be a fee to visit sick people?"

He made a big fuss about that and hung up, saying "God bless you, Bruno. God bless you."

I went to the hospital and visited with the patients and it went well. Then I took the guy aside that I'd talked to on the phone and told him, "Hey, you know you kind of insulted me the other day...asking about a fee for coming up here."

He apologized and said, "Well, you wouldn't know this, but we originally had four baseball players scheduled and they held us up at the last minute. They each wanted quite a bit of money to show up or else they told us to forget it. We certainly didn't have the kind of money they wanted so that was that with the baseball players."

"We had already told the patients that we were going to be getting some important guests and when the baseball players pulled this, we didn't want to let our people down. We knew that a lot of them watched wrestling and when we mentioned the name of Bruno Sammartino, they all seemed to be your fans. We thought that if we could contact you, it would save the day. And it certainly did."

When he told me about what had happened, I got very angry. I thought to myself whether it's me the wrestler or some other athlete in football, baseball, basketball, hockey...you name the sport...here we are...healthy, doing what we enjoy the most in life and getting paid very well for it. So how can anyone with a scrap of decency in them demand to be paid to visit patients at a Veteran's Hospital? This I cannot understand. Never in a million years.

I was more than happy to be able to put some joy into the lives of some Vets.

Even though I've been telling you about what mixed feelings that I might have for certain athletes and entertainers that I've met, let me also mention that there have been times when I've lost respect for the fans...not all of them of course, but for the lunatics that hang out on the fringe of fandom.

Often, people have asked me which opponent I feared the most in the ring. In all seriousness, I have never come up against any opponent who has ever struck fear in my heart as much as what I've seen some fans try to pull.

One time I was wrestling Big Bill Miller, who was, if you remember, six foot seven and weighed 320 pounds. Well, we were going at it one evening and all of a sudden we both heard a fracas commence just three or four rows back from the ring. We saw police running in from every direction and fans were hollering and grabbing at one guy in particular. Turned out he had a gun inside a hollowed-out book and he had come to kill Bill Miller. His hate for Miller as a wrestler had tipped his mental balance into the crazy zone.

Just as he was pulling out his pistol to fire, a man next to him saw it and grabbed his wrist, then started screaming for help. He held on to the gunman for dear life until the police could come and haul this nut away.

Another time, I was wrestling Waldo Von Eric at the Boston Gardens, an arena that has a strange shape to it with sections of seats rising nearly straight up into the ceiling. As we were circling around the ring, I felt something whiz by my head. It crashed to the mat with a horrible sound.

Entering the ring was a new experience each time. You just never knew if there might be a crazed fan in the crowd.

180

We stopped and looked and saw the object was a huge padlock. Considering the distance it had traveled, the lock had generated enough momentum to have killed either me or Von Eric instantly. Luckily, the irate fan's aim was off that night.

I've also witnessed matches where a fan has stormed the ring, waving a knife in the air, overcome with anger to such an extent that the only thing on his mind is to maim and kill. In Oklahoma City, Angelo Sevoldi was wrestling Denny Hodge, a former Olympian. Angelo was getting the best of Denny when Denny's father got carried away and jumped into the ring to defend his son's honor. The frustrated father sliced Angelo's back with a knife, slitting the skin from Angel's shoulders down below his waist. Sevoldi survived somehow, ending up with over two hundred stitches and one of the nastiest scars you'll ever want to see.

Black Jack Mulligan faced a fan in Boston who charged into the ring with a hunting knife. As Mulligan tried to get away, the fan slashed him in the thigh then continued to drag the knife along the complete length of his upper leg.

Sonny Meyers had a fan open him up by sticking a knife into his stomach. Sonny had to hold onto his own guts as they were falling out and run to the dressing room to get away from this jerk. A doctor rushed in right away and saved Sonny's life.

A wrestler can also find himself endangered simply from the fans' enthusiasm for you. When I won the title from Buddy Rogers, the crowd's reaction had me literally fighting for my life. Although the fans meant well, they didn't realize that twenty thousand people pushing, shoving, grabbing and moving in the same direction can be deadly. I'll tell you I've never felt so helpless during circumstances like that and there's nothing you can do because the mob is so huge. In the heat of the moment, the fans don't realize that their behavior is not only dangerous to the person they are cheering, but also dangerous to themselves. We have even had fans drop over from heart attacks, scared to death by being caught in the middle of this kind of demonstration.

Granted, most of the fans are well behaved but there are always some who get carried away in the excitement. As a wrestler, when you see incidents like these happen again and again, you really do get jumpy...and more than a little leary. Whenever I stepped into the ring, I always tried to block those memories out in order to concentrate on the match. But there were always those nagging thoughts.

One wrestler who never failed to draw the ire of the fans was Fred Blassie. Whenever Blassie and I would hold a match, attendance always zoomed.

Blassie was the rule-breaker, tough as nails with a reputation for ferocious behavior. He was mean, rugged and a winner.

When you wrestled Blassie, you could expect anything. If he could hurt you, he would. If the match was going badly for Blassie, he'd go for an eye or sneak in a low blow to stop you. And to him everybody was a pencil-necked geek. He didn't care who he was talking to, if you got in his way you were a pencil-necked geek. Blassie even went so far as to record a song called "Pencil-Necked Geek" which you can still find on those compilation albums of "worst-ever" music that D.J. Doctor Demento puts out.

I wrestled Blassie in arenas all over the country and in fact, we sold out Madison Square Garden several times. The one match that I remember most vividly took place at an outdoor baseball park in New Jersey. That night we set an attendance record. That was because the fans were there in full force with nothing on their minds but letting Blassie know how much they hated him.

Toward the end of our match that night, I was handling Blassie well and Freddie knew he was coming up short. He reached back and walloped his fist into me way, way below the belt. I fell to my knees from the pain and tried to clear my head. That's when pandemonium broke out.

The fans were outraged by Blassie's illegal shot. Within seconds, chairs started flying into the ring, all aimed at Blassie's head. Then the crowd pressed around the ring and started shaking the posts, whipping the ropes back and forth wildly. Blassie stood in the center, clenching his fists and shouting that he was ready to take on anybody.

The police charged in and attempted to break up the melee with no immediate success. They called for reinforcements and even requested that some of the other wrestlers help them get Blassie out of danger. But no matter what the police tried for a while the fans held Blassie hostage. Chairs rained in from every direction and I remember hugging the mat, trying to keep from being hit. Eventually, police and wrestlers formed a human circle around Blassie and escorted him out the park.

Now let me tell you about one wrestler whom I didn't like at all years ago. In fact, I considered him a pushy, arrogant loudmouth. As the years have rolled by though, I have come to admire and respect him. In every sense of the word, he's a good and decent man.

I'm referring to Lou Albano, somebody you probably recognize from the movies and from his appearances with pop singer Cyndi Lauper in her early MTV videos. Recently, he's been doing a TV series called 'The Super Mario Brothers' in which he plays Mario the plumber. Well, Lou started out with the rest of us years ago in the wrestling business and he certainly has come a long way from the wild, rowdy guy he once was.

Lou was born in Rome, but was brought to the United States when he was only three months old. His father became a well-known New York City physician and his mother was a concert pianist.

What most folks don't remember about Lou is what a great, all-around athlete he was. In college, he made his mark in football, receiving a full scholarship to play for Tennessee.

One unfortunate side to Lou's early career was his temper. He ended up attending quite a few more universities after Tennessee. His off-the-field behavior drew him into lots of street and bar fights, which led to his dismissal from Tennessee and other colleges along the way. Since he was such a talented football player, different schools would pick him up until he got into trouble again. Then Lou would just pack his bags and move on. Finally, even Lou got tired of the vagabond life and he dropped out of school for good.

Lou started wrestling professionally two or three years before I did. I remember him as a guy who loved to hang out in bars you wouldn't want to be caught dead in.

If somebody would say the wrong thing to him, which was easy enough to do, he'd become an absolute maniac and clear the place out. Lou was a tough customer, the type of guy who'd have to be knocked unconscious before he'd stop fighting.

As a wrestler, some of his bar brawling assets turned into liabilities in the ring. He never really reached any great plateau as a pro wrestler and I'm sure he would agree with that judgement.

What set Lou apart from the crowd is that he took his ring knowledge, built on that with his gutsy, fearless style and became the most successful manager of wrestling talent in the history of the industry. He's developed people who have become champions both individually and on tag teams...winning seventeen championships in all.

Lou's great gift is his knack for bluffing and for brinksmanship. He would scream and yell at his wrestlers and demand, cajole and order that they do exactly as he told them. He also had his own way with the promoters, lobbying non-stop on behalf of his own roster, demanding that his people get better television time, better matches, better ring appearances. That was the Lou I didn't care for at all.

Let me tell you what changed my mind about Lou Albano. When Lou was managing talent for the WWF, back when Vince McMahon, Sr. was running the show, Lou complied with all the rules, did everything he was obligated to do and the situation was fine. When Vince, Jr. took over, Lou was faced with making a career decision which went against the wishes of the WWF. In short, Lou was offered a major role in a movie called, 'The Wise Guys,' which was to co-star him with Danny DeVito and Joe Piscopo. It was a great break.

However, Vince, Jr. didn't want Lou to make the movie unless Lou asked the permission of the WWF. If he just would do this, then they would give their blessing and everything would be rosy.

Lou's attitude was, "Hey, look...I do what I'm supposed to do for the WWF. I don't need anybody's permission for anything. How I spend my own free time is my business"

That didn't sit too well with Vince, Jr. Eventually, the WWF gave Lou the ultimatum that if he did this movie without their permission, then he was through with them...for good. To his credit, Lou didn't blink an eye the way most guys might have. He broke with the WWF and went ahead to make 'The Wise Guys.' The success of that film led to many other roles including a movie called, 'Body Slam', appearances in different TV series like 'Miami Vice' and as I mentioned earlier, he's now involved with the 'Super Mario Brothers.'

What ultimately has made me a Lou Albano fan is his involvement with charity, particularly with the fight to combat Multiple Sclerosis. Lou gives so much of himself and of his time, traveling all over the country as a spokesperson for this worthy cause. Of course, he doesn't receive any pay, at best only plane fare and hotel reimbursements. Lou has sacrificed a lot personally to dedicate himself to raising money to fight this deadly disease.

THOUGHTS ABOUT TODAY'S WRESTLERS

In my day, the only bad habits that I can remember some wrestlers may have had was a liking for the bottle a little bit too much. That certainly isn't a very good thing for an athlete to get involved with.

But that's nothing compared to what happens today. What really got ugly in this profession, besides the bizarre circus atmosphere, has been the use and abuse of steroids and other drugs. Wrestling has become infiltrated with drugs and it pains me tremendously to see this profession, that was so good to me, become what it is today.

Tragically, many current wrestlers are on the stuff and have serious health problems as a result of it. Only God knows what deaths will occur as a result of these anabolic steroids.

And it's not only the steroids. What I say next is something that I realize many people will be angry about but it's fact. There are many more illegal drugs being fooled around with than just the steroids. I'm talking about cocaine and marijuana and pills of every different kind that you can imagine.

The real irony is that certain promoters have tried to give us this nonsense that the wrestlers are all being tested for drugs before they can compete. Well, it's all nonsense.

Only the promoter himself has access to the results. There's no committee anywhere to look at the results and then intervene if they had to.

What happens is that if some guy who's low on the totem pole shows positive, they make an example of him by giving him a three-week suspension. But if one of the top guns is hooked, since he's featured all over the country as a top attraction, the positive test will never be reported.

As far as I'm concerned, there's no legitimate drug testing because for it to be legitimate, there would have to be supervision by a body that's independent from wrestling, like a State Athletic Commission. It's all a charade.

I think if the general public knew how much of this was going on today in wrestling by some of these so-called heroes that the children are rooting for that they would be shocked and devastated by it all.

I personally have strong, strong resentments of that. I know myself that there were times when I was asked to put on the tights, not just because somebody got hurt, but because somebody didn't pass their drug testing. This occurred as late as 1984 after I had been retired for several years. And again, these were the little fish who could be replaced. No problem.

But there were much bigger fish out there whose test results were only

I'm proud to say that I never used or condoned the use of steroids.

seen by one man, the big boss, the promoter. Drug testing is a joke...and the problems are still growing.

I'm often asked how I feel about the quality of today's wrestling. Well, in the WWF unfortunately, I see very little talent in wrestling skills. There may be some wrestlers with above average abilities, but they are very, very few.

On the other hand, there's the National Wrestling Alliance and they do impress me. They have some real athletes in this league who have had solid amateur experience and who are now tremendous pros.

They have guys like the Steiner Brothers from Michigan...national champions. They have Mike Rotundo, out of Syracuse, an all-American. Steve Williams from Oklahoma is another tremendous wrestler. The list goes on and on.

So, particularly in the NWA, there's no question that there is some good wrestling out there. The downside is that wrestling in general has lost whatever credibility it ever had.

This has happened I believe because of what the WWF did to wrestling. Now I was involved with the WWF for many years and really believed in it. When Vince McMahon, Sr. was running it, it had become the Number One wrestling organization in the world.

Well, when Vince McMahon, Jr. succeeded his father, the cartoon characters took over. Just think of the wrestlers that they've developed like the Ultimate Warrior. Here's a guy who's painted up, with long hair and wears straps on his arms.

Then there's the crazy outfits they wear to portray an image. For example, you have the Honky Tonk Man who imitates Elvis Presley in the ring.

And there's Hulk Hogan (I don't know who he imitates) whose character is geared toward kids and merchandising. The kids see Hulk Hogan and they run to Mom and Dad to get them to buy them this toy or this headband or that calendar or any of the other hundreds of junk items they're selling.

I see them doing this strictly for the Almighty Dollar. Don't get me wrong. Everybody's in business to succeed and make money but what the WWF has done is to stick the actual wrestling, the match itself, into dead last on the priority list. Professional wrestling desperately needs better quality people in that organization, people with legitimate wrestling skills.

Adults have lost complete faith in wrestling. Grownups don't go to the arenas anymore and as a result, a league like the National Wrestling Alliance, even with the tremendous wrestlers that they have, can't attract the crowds. You see, the NWA doesn't have the cartoon characters that attract the children like the WWF.

Today, Mom and Dad takes little Joey and little Susan and little Michael to see the WWF characters that the children see on television. And what really is happening is that the WWF doesn't get the large crowds anyway, except for an occasional event. They're not doing all that well.

Well, I think that the sideshow atmosphere with the snakes and the parrots and the dogs, the painted faces and the costumes from Mars will attract a certain percentage of the kids who will drag their parents to these spectacles, but sad to say, there's no credibility left to my sport.

Many of the fans who talk to me say what a joke wrestling has become. And as more and more people talk that way, then the question becomes: What about the future of wrestling?

Well, when when the head of the WWF sees that wrestling's no longer profitable, he can get involved in some other business or he can just retire. But what happens to the would-be wrestler? What happens to the young guy who trains hard and wants to become a wrestler when nobody believes in it any more?

This is the tragedy of wrestling today. The NWA is trying to keep wrestling legitimate but I feel that because of the WWF's much larger national coverage, they have overshadowed the NWA. Now most people judge wrestling only by what they see with the WWF.

What I hope for is that eventually the children who are the fans today will grow up and leave behind the nonsense. The adults already don't support wrestling like they used to. Maybe the WWF should read the hand-writing on the wall and seek other business ventures.

Then it will be up to somebody to bring back true wrestling that starts with the basics. Enough gimmicks!

I really feel very sad about wrestling today. In a way, I'm very angry because this is the game that I have hurt my body for. I have had a lot of serious injuries, but I believed in my sport. I always gave my very, very best.

I'm not suggesting that I was the only one who did that either. There were other great guys in this game who also gave it everything they had. It's just that I had sincerely wished that once I retired, wrestling would be looked upon with the same respect as baseball, football or any other major sport. Instead, look what happened!

I suppose it will take a long time for the credibility to return because those fans who have lost their faith in the sport will probably never regain it. Hopefully, there will be new fans who will someday get to see good wrestling and they will like it and then wrestling will be reborn.

This process will take years but I do believe that the sport will come back and come back strong. Wrestling will never die. It's been here forever and it will be here forever.

FINAL THOUGHTS, FINAL SHOTS

During my career, I've known what it is to be in the spotlight. Yet sometimes that spotlight gives off such a glare that you can't see clearly. The trick is to be able to stand up under the unblinking beam of fame and still walk away a winner. That's the ultimate challenge. Two groups of winners that I've admired for their graciousness under fire have been boxers and believe it or not operatic stars.

Let's talk about opera first. Opera people have long owned the reputation for being temperamental, but of all the people I've met in show business, opera stars have impressed me the most...even despite their volatile personalities.

I've maintained a life-long love for opera. Whenever I met and chatted with opera stars, each one was always very open with me. Of course, I never had the chance to see them with their public so I can't judge them in that sense. But in their contacts with me, these stars displayed none of the bad manners that gossip columnists write about in the tabloids.

Two names that come to mind as being particularly thoughtful and kind were first, Renata Tabaldi. Renata was actually a big wrestling fan and when we met, she acted like I was the big star instead of her. The second name was Giovanni Avila, a gentleman who had actually been Caruso's pianist. Ever since I met Avila on one of my tours of Australia, I would seek him out whenever I returned. During my visits, we would sit and discuss Caruso and his life. Avila would share unpublished and rare photographs of Caruso and himself in appearances all over the world.

The one man who had opened the door for me to this world of opera was not only a boxing and wrestling promoter, but also an opera impressario...Orelio Tabbiani. Orelio and I took a great liking for each other. Since we were both native Italians, we spoke the mother tongue all the time we were together.

Through Orelio, I met greats like Mario Delmonaco, one of the most highly regarded dramatic tenors of all time; and Guiseppe Distefano, one of the greatest lyrical tenors who ever appeared on stage. Of course, I don't want to forget Franco Corelli, a singer with whom I got to be close friends.

Corelli absolutely used to blow my mind when he sang. When he hit a high C, his power and breath control were phenomenal. His range was just incredible. Franco was a spindo, which meant that he could sing dramatic as well as lyrical roles. Whenever you spelled out his name on the marquee at the New York Met for example, the program would be sold out

189

immediately.

Some years ago the Lincoln Center was about to introduce a new French opera and Rudolph Bing, the Center's director, and others there felt that only Corelli should introduce this new work to New York City. Bing felt that Corelli, who was at this point the greatest opera star in the world, was the one star who could unfold the music's magic for the audience.

Well, politics run deep even in the world of opera. Nicholi Getta, a Russian tenor, had already made a recording of the work, and Getta had his core of admirers inside the Met who wanted him and not Corelli to perform in the New York debut. The in-fighting got so ugly that Getti supporters let it be known that if Corelli showed up for opening night, he would have his legs broken for his trouble.

Corelli, even speaking no English, picked right up on the seriousness of the threats and panicked, saying he wasn't going to risk life and limb for a French opera. Corelli was assured that extra policemen would be hired to protect him. He responded by saying that he was fearful his attackers

Not even singing lessons from the great Corelli could help me.

190

would dress up like a policeman to get at him.

Then one of Corelli's people remembered that Bruno Sammartino was a big Corelli fan. With Corelli's permission, his people called me and explained the situation. I readily agreed to stand guard over Corelli throughout the first performance. He was my favorite opera singer. How could I turn down such genius?

As backup, I contacted two wrestling friends of mine, Tony Marino and Willie Farkus. Together the three of us would serve as Corelli's first line of defense.

I assured Corelli he had nothing to worry about. The show must go on.

The day of the scheduled opening, I flew to New York and went directly to Corelli's apartment on 57th Street. After promising him that everything was going to be taken care of, I escorted the trembling tenor to Lincoln Center and walked him down the long hallway to his dressingroom. While makeup artists transformed the Italian superstar into a Frenchman for the night, I hovered around the building, checking the halls and doorways, making sure that no unsavory characters lurked about. Then I followed at his side, step by step, until he reached the wings. Before he went on, I pointed out Marino and Farkus seated in the first row, who were in effect securing the safety of the front of the stage.

I told Corelli to sing freely. He had nothing to worry about. I would be backstage and my two friends would be right up front in case anyone stormed the performance. Corelli took a deep breath and thanked me. When he went on, his singing was so phenomenal that at times he made me forget why I was backstage in the first place.

At any rate, nothing happened. No opera terrorists charging the stage. No broken legs. Just pure unadulterated opera.

After the program, I stayed with him in his dressingroom while he climbed out of makeup and changed back into his street clothes. Then I rode back with him to his apartment and turned him over to security guards that he had hired to watch him through the rest of the night. The very next day he was flying to Milan to appear in an opera there, so once out of New York, he would be safe. As I shook his hand and was getting ready to leave, his thanks poured out. Corelli had become the happiest man alive just then because thanks to Bruno and friends, his legs had stayed intact.

Another group that I enjoyed being around might at first seem far removed from the world of opera. For me, the connecting rod between the two was their dedication to excellence. I'm talking about boxers...men who trained hard, worked hard, took punishment and gave it out...mostly just for the love of the sport.

My appreciation of boxing, like my enthusiasm for opera, started early in life. When I was wrestling as an amatuer, I would either be at the Pitt Field House with the college men or over at the Y where a ring was maintained. The Y was home to a super, super guy named Al Quale, a great boxer in his own right, who had retired from pugilism and became a policeman. All still kept his hand in the fighting game by teaching kids how to box. Sone of his charges became golden glove champions and a few even turned pro right out of the Oakland Y. I remember Quale as a great light heavyweight, second only to the legendary Billy Conn.

Al always used to pester me, saying, "Bruno, what are you doing with that wrestling? Boxing...that's where it's at You should be a fighter and make all the money."

One time just to please Al, because really I had no interest in actually turning into a boxer, I started to shadow box around the ring. In a short time Al had moved me over to the bag and I hit that for a while, and the before long, Al had me sparring with different partners.

My heart was in wrestling and not in boxing but in order to please Al, I kept working out as a boxer for some time. Of course, when he'd leave the building, back I'd go to wrestling.

Finally, Al thought I had progressed in my boxing skills to the extent where he insisted on taking me to Stillman's Gym in New York City. There he introduced me to some real giants in the world of boxing promotion. Guys like Vic Marsell, Whitey Beepsting and Ernie Barracha took a close look at me as a boxing prospect because Al had put out the good word on me As I waltzed around the ring in Stillman's Gym, sparring with one or two of the local boys, I kept thinking to myself, "What in the world am I doing? This isn't me."

Believe me, the guys they gave me to spar with were the real thing...heavyweights who knew what they were doing. It didn't take long for me to get the worst of it. One thing in my favor though...nobody ever put me down. I could take a whale of a punch. Now, at the time I didn't know if that was good or bad for a boxer, but I took some incredible blows. Afterward, the guys told me it wasn't a good idea. It's great to be able to absorb punishment, but one main principle in boxing is to give and then duck, not to give and take.

Everybody was supportive, and the suggestion was made that I get a job at the New York docks and come to Stillman's on a daily basis to continue my training in boxing. At that point, I had to call a halt. I confessed that wrestling was the sport that had the number one spot in my heart. I thanked everyone for their interest in me, then told them that I had to fly back to Pittsburgh to return to my true passion...wrestling.

Even though I passed on a shot at professional boxing, I've kept a fan's lifelong interest in the sport. Thanks to my role as a professional wrestler, I've had the chance to talk with many of the boxing greats. Every boxing champion that I met seemed down to earth and very considerate to friends and fans alike. To me boxers are a wonderful breed.

In the late Fifties and early Sixties, boxing's middleweight division was at its peak, heralding the toughest competition in history. Names like Gill Turner, Bobby Boyd, Willy Troy and Rory Calhoun may not ring a bell today but back then these guys were all championship caliber.

One boxer who fought them all and eventually defeated Tiger for the crown was Joey Giardello. I met Joey right after he worn the middleweight championship and I was very impressed with his level-headed nature. Joey was one of the very best and as proof of this, I only have to remember the whipping that he laid on Sugar Ray Robinson.

193

Then there was Tony DeMarca, a man they called the Little Rocky Marciano. Toney was known as THE knockout artist and I used to love to watch him go to work. Two of the greatest fights I've ever seen in my life were his bout and rematch with Carmine Basillia.

Of course, I couldn't forget Smokin' Joe Frazier, a tremendous champion in the heavyweight class. Yet if you talk to Joe about the fight game and who was the best in his opinion, he'd always point to Joe Lewis and Rocky Marciano as his picks for greatness. Joe was a humble man who never boasted about who he could beat or who he could smash to a pulp.

Tough Guys...Sammartino and Fraser clown for the camera.

I met Mohammad Ali a couple of times and I wish I could say that I hold him in the same regard as I do the other boxers I've mentioned. Without question, he was an accomplished fighter yet he had this need to put himself above everyone else. Maybe a lot of what he babbled on about was just a put on...but for me, the bottom line was this...there's just no way he would have beaten Joe Lewis or Rocky Marciano in their prime.

I got to be friends with Jake LaMotta, the man whose story was told in the movie "Raging Bull." Jake was one of the toughest middleweights to ever walk the streets yet if you talk with him, he's one of the funniest guys you'll ever meet. In fact, he makes a nice living these day appearing in night clubs as a comedian. His wisecracks and jokes will bring tears to your eyes.

Rocky Graziano, another middleweight champion, recorded some of the most memorable fights in boxing history, taking on the likes of the great Tony Zale. Out of the ring, Graziano, too, is one of the nicest guys you'll ever meet.

Hey, who's leading anyway?

Two other boxers who I got to know personally were Willie Pep and Jersey Joe Wolcott. Willie worked with the State Athletic Commission in Connecticut. When I'd see him, I'd ask him to tell me about his fights. He loved to tell the stories and was always very thoughtful when a fan like myself would ask questions about certain fights.

I got to know Jersey Joe because he refereed many of my matches. Jersey

Joe is unquestionably one of the sweetest human beings on the face of the earth.

One time in Madison Square Garden a promoter came up to me just before my match was to begin and said, "Bruno, everybody knows you're a big fan of boxing. We got this kid, Nino Benvenuti, coming in from Italy. He's going to be training in the Catskills and what he'd like most is to meet you. I guess he read all about you in the Italian papers and magazines.

I said, "Sure, I'd love to meet him. As a matter of fact, I've been reading all about him, too!"

A week or so later, I flew into New York early one morning and drove out to the Catskills to Nino's training camp. Since my match wasn't until later that evening, I had plenty of time to get there and spend a few hours with the young challenger.

When I shook hands with Benvenuti, he seemed in awe of my physique. He said he couldn't believe how big and muscled I was in person. I guess at that time I weighed in aroung 275 pounds.

The publicity man had me take off my shirt and they they took a couple of pictures of Nino and me doing road work. Later, we even sparred a couple of rounds in the ring. Nino complemented me, saying that I had good, quick hands.

Nino introduced me to all of his family that he had brought with him to the training camp. Everything in the camp was aimed at making him feel right at home. He said he really missed his parents.

Then I watched him train for a while. He seemed to go into a trance as he worked so intense was his concentration. He wanted to be champion so very much.

Later, Nino expressed curiousity about me and my training. He wanted to know how I could weight 275 pounds and still be in the shape that I was in? He was puzzled by my stamina and speed. When we were running or sparring in the ring, Nino expected my arms to drop off since my biceps, triceps and forearms were so well developed. Instead, he saw that I kept at a good speed and didn't tire out.

I explained to him that wrestling was a fantastic conditioner. I told him that when you wrestle daily and with some of the matches lasting an hour or more, you ended up in great shape. That boggled his mind. Then he wanted to know how after a wrestler gets bodyslammed or thrown from the ring, can we jump up and keep going...without pads or protection of any kind. He wanted to know if there was a trick to it.

I said, "Nino...how can there be a trick to somebody picking you up, taking you over their head and then smashing you to the mat? You boxers

Nino and Bruno enjoy sharing an Italian newspaper.

197

use the same ring as we use. You know there's no trick to being a good boxer. You've just got to be in the best possible condition that you can."

Nino appreciated that argument. I went on to say, "As a fighter, how many body shots can you take? You know that depends on your conditioning. The average fan out there can't really relate to a body shot. They see the head shots and see the head jerk back and know that the fighter has gotten hurt...but as professional athletes, we both know that body shots can be even more devastating if you aren't in shape."

The longer Nino and I talked, the more I felt like I was being interviewed by a newspaperman. He was so open...curious about so many things. What I remember best though about Nino was his professional dedication...and his pride in all things Italian. Whenever Nino saw an Italian succeeding in any sport, he would always make an effort to acknowledge that person. He never lost his love of country.

The first time Nino Benvenuti fought Griffith he lost. A few short months later, he bounced right back and fought Griffith again, this time beat him and taking the title. Nino held the crown for quite some time until he was defeated by the Argentinian Monzone.

One name that I certainly don't want to forget is Rocky Marciano, someone who I considered a very good friend. His real name was Rocco Marciano and his family came from the same province in Italy that I did. Shortly before Rocky was killed in a plane crash in Iowa, I met with him to talk about a South African tour that I was to be making that year. Rocky wanted to join us as a guest referee, a role that he had filled in some of my earlier bouts. His death was a tragic waste.

But you know, sports figures, entertainers, all those people who must travel, run that extra risk. Although they say each time you board a plane, your risk of dying in a crash is less overall than if you were riding in a car, the more miles you log in the air, the closer the odds come together.

Traveling was always one of the most frustrating things for me. When I first won the title, I had an incredibly hectic schedule. I wrestled six days one week, took a day off, then wrestled seven days the next week. Then I'd start the fourteen day cycle again...one day off every two weeks. The reason I had to spend the second Sunday of this cycle wrestling was because of the promise I had made to Frank Tunney in Toronto. There was no way I was going to back out on my agreement with Frank to come to Toronto every two weeks. He had been very decent to me, giving me a chance to earn a living when I'd been suspended in the United States.

The problem that this created for me though was formidable. I could only make it back to Pittsburgh to see my family every two weeks. And you'd be surprised how many times that I'd be flying in from New York and the airport would be closed because of the bad winter weather. Then we'd have to fly on to Chicago or Omaha and land there. By the time the Pittsburgh airport would reopen, I'd have to catch a plane to head toward my Monday wrestling engagement. I'd spend a whole day running between planes and airports and I'd never make it home.

Besides keeping my commitment to Frank Tunney, I had to make myself available for live television interviews on Channel 11 in Pittsburgh. These live shots were very important tools for the promoters and they insisted that I appear on air on a regular basis to talk about upcoming bouts at the Civic Arena.

Talk about scrambling. Here might be a typical scenario for my TV appearances. The promoters would book me for an interview late in the afternoon and at the same time commit me to wrestle later that night in Philadelphia. Since the TV spot would air live, I couldn't pre-tape it and duck out to the airport so I had to hang in there until they were ready for me and then, more often than not, it would be so late that there would be no commercial flights left to Philly.

That meant the promoters would have to charter a single-engine Cessna for me. I'd finish my interview, head for the airport, climb into this lawn mower with wings and it'd be me and the pilot buzzing across Pennsylvania in an attempt to reach Philadelphia in time for my late night wrestling match.

Those planes were no bargain, let me tell you. Once I was flying to Philly in weather so bad that with every lurch of the plane, I was thinking, "Oh, my God. This is it!".

Ray the pilot had such an intense look on his face that I was far from reassured about my safety. When we finally reached the outskirts of Philadelphia after what seemed like an eternity, the tower told us that the airport was closed. Ray pleaded with them that he had to make an emergency landing, and so with sense of urgency conveyed, the tower gave him permission to try one.

All I can say about that landing was that we both walked away from it. The plane hit the runway terrifically hard, spun and flipped over onto its side. The force of this broke the wing clean away.

I had a similar experience flying from Windsor, Ontario to Indianapolis. After a television interview in Windsor, I headed to my next wrestling engagement in Indiana. Again, this was a charter flight with just me and the pilot stuffed into what appeared to be a flying phone booth. As we approached the Indianapolis airport, we found that bad weather had shut down all of their runways. I listened to the pilot discuss our situation with the tower.

Bill Cardille was the host of WIIC-TV's Studio Wrestling in Pittsburgh. That's him on the left with the great Baseball Hall of Famer Pie Traynor in the center.

It seemed that we couldn't fly on the the next available airport because we were running out of fuel.

The tower finally declared that we were an emergency and told the pilot to try and put the plane down on Runway 4. The weather had now socked everything in to the extent that it seemed as if the windshield had a layer of cotton gauze over it. You could see nothing but rain and fog and clouds.

We descended for the longest time, then suddenly trees appeared right below the wheels. I'd swear we touched the tops of them. Then all at once we saw the end of the runway...very close. The plane slammed so hard into the concrete that we shot up into the air again. The pilot circled and made a second attempt at a landing.

Again, a downdraft hammered us and the plane bounced up...but this time, instead of circling for a third try, the pilot persisted. He aimed us right at the middle of the runway and brought the wheels back to earth once more. The aircraft pogo-sticked up and down two more times and now we were running out of real estate.

To avoid diving off the end of the runway and plunging down a steep embankment, at the last second the pilot swerved the plane to his extreme right into a grassy field. As soon as the wheels left concrete and hit dirt, the plane up-ended itself and flipped over several times. Again, both myself and the pilot climbed out of the wreckage unhurt.

After that one, I told the promoters NO MORE LITTLE PLANES! I told them to schedule my interviews well in advance of my matches. I refused to risk my neck just for some five minute interview. And that was that.

The truth of the matter is that I've had some close calls on the big birds, too. But you cannot be a champion wrestler and not fly. In the old days, wrestlers took the train. Why not? If you only had one or two matches a week, why not take your time in getting there? The modern era brought in the match-a-night pace. There was no other way to handle it than by flying.

Once I remember flying out of Boston in a four-engine prop driven plane. We were on our way back to Pittsburgh. I was sitting about halfway back next to Father Rocco, whom I had bumped into at the airport. I had met him some years ago at an opera. He was a wrestling fan and as we both shared a love for opera, we had become friends. Since he spoke little or no English, he was pleased to find out that we were booked on the same flight. Now he had someone to talk to.

After we took off, Father Rocco turned to his Bible and began reading. I respected his wish for quiet reflection and I began to reflect myself...only I started to become aware that something was wrong with the plane. The aircraft seemed to be struggling, waddling through the sky. I glanced out into the night but couldn't make out anything. Then I realized that the engines weren't making as much noise as usual.

I quietly excused myself and headed for the back where I recognized one of the stewardessess. I flew so much in those days that I was a familiar figure in the air so she knew me right away, too. I whispered to her, "You know I've been flying too long not to know that something's up. Can you tell me what's going on?".

She told me as quietly as possible, "Well, Bruno, we're not supposed to say anything, but three engines have conked out.".

I said out loud, "Three!" then quickly lowered my voice again, "Three?".

"Yes, but we don't want to make a big deal out of it. We've already turned around and are headed back to Boston. We can still make it on one engine with no trouble," she reassured me.

I thanked her and returned to my seat. Father Rocco was still reading his Bible. He looked up at me and smiled and I smiled back, thinking, "Please, keep reading that Bible of yours! Don't stop reading for anything!".

Well, we made it back to Boston okay and Father Rocco and the rest of the passengers never knew what had happened. The pilot just announced that they were having some difficulties and had to return to Boston to transfer us to another aircraft. Everybody moaned and groaned, but I thanked our lucky stars for that one good engine...and Father Rocco's Bible.

I remember one time in the early Seventies that I nearly went to Boston on a connecting flight from Montreal to Philadelphia and it was only the luck of the draw that kept me off that plane. Because of bad weather throughout the Northeast, flights were being canceled and rerouted all night long. So when I reached the Montreal airport, my direct flight to Philadelphia had been canceled.

The ticket attendant who greeted me with this news scanned his screen and said, "Bruno, here's the best I can do. I can fly you from Montreal to Boston then change you over there on a flight to Philadelphia. It's a little roundabout but better than spending the night sleeping in a chair here, right?"

I shrugged and said, "Okay. Let's do that."

He arranged my ticket, handed me my new flight envelope and wished me well. I got on the phone and called Vince McMahon at the Philadelphia Arena and told him that I was probably going to be late for my match because my original flight had been canceled. Then I told him the airline had booked me into Boston where I'd have to catch a connecting flight into Philly. With the weather the way it was, I told him I couldn't predict when I'd arrive. In his usual style, Vince told me to get there the best way I could and he'd see me at the Arena.

I hung up the phone, then just as I was walking away to get to the right gate, the attendant called out, "Bruno! Bruno, come on back!"

I hurried over to see what he wanted. He told me a flight that was headed for Philadelphia has landed briefly at the Montreal airpot. It had been rerouted through Montreal because of the lousy weather all up and down the Lakes. And there was one seat left on it. "Did you want to take it?" he asked.

Of course I said yes. I'll take a direct flight any day. So we changed my ticket one more time. I was scratched off the flight to Boston and penciled in on the straight shot to Philly. I rushed to claim my seat on that flight. Of course, I didn't have enough time to call McMahon back to tell him of my second change of plans.

When I walked into the Arena in Philadelphia, Phil Zacko, who was one of McMahon's partners, took one look at me and I thought he was going to faint. It was like he had just seen a ghost.

I said, "Phil, what's the matter?"

He squinted and said, "Bruno, it's really you!"

"Sure it's me, Phil. What's wrong with you?" I thought maybe Phil had temporarily lost his mind.

Phil stammered, "My God, Bruno. We just heard on the news that that flight you told us you were on...you know, the one from Montreal to Boston. It crashed trying to land in the storm...exploded on impact...burned to ashes. No survivors. Nobody."

I couldn't believe it. "Crashed?"

Phil grabbed my arm and twisted it, making sure that I really was there. "But what happened? Vince said you called him. Told him you had to take that Boston flight to get to Philly."

I explained that last minute switch to Phil. All I could think of was, "My God...all those poor people."

Let me tell you one more airplane story and I'll get off this. Once I was touring Australia. On this particular day I wrestled in Brisbane then returned to my hotel room, knowing that I had to get up early the next morning to catch a 7:45 a.m. flight to Sidney. The promoter had booked me on the earliest available plane because I had to do a TV interview at 11 a.m.

No matter where I've traveled around the world, I've always brought my own little alarm clock as a backup for the hotel's wakeup call. Too many times the front desk has failed to call me on time or even at all. When you wake up in the morning and already you're an hour behind schedule that makes the whole day pretty traumatic.

Anyway, just as I was about to crawl into bed, I set my own alarm for 6:00 a.m., called the front desk and asked them for a wakeup call for the same time and went to sleep. Actually, I seem to have my own built-in alarm clock and I usually wake up on my own, just a few minutes before the alarm's set to go off.

Well, the next morning nothing happened. The alarm didn't go off. The front desk didn't call. And I didn't wake up until 8:00 a.m. I was furious and I called downstairs, asking that they get me a cab right away. Maybe my flight had been delayed, and I still could make it. I got dressed, didn't even brush my teeth, checked out and jumped into a cab.

We careened out to the airport and I found out that the flight I had been booked on had indeed taken off on time. The plane had crashed on takeoff, plunged into the earth and blew up in a monstrous explosion. Everyone died.

This match might never have taken place if I hadn't switched flights.

People have asked me, "Do you think you have a Guardian Angel hanging over your shoulder?"

I suppose I've thought about that as I've gotten older. I stop to remember the close calls and sometimes it does give me the chills for an instant. But I still got on that next plane to Sydney. You have to keep going. You have to fulfill your obligations. That's what it is to be a professional, no matter what you do.

Of course, I think about those people who didn't make it. Did they have Guardian Angels, too? If so, was it just their time to pass over?

Or maybe it was just the luck of the draw. I don't know. I have a hard time defining luck.

Was I lucky to have survived the hazards of World War II? If I had been lucky, maybe I would have been born in another time and in another place. Was it luck that when I broke my neck, I wasn't completely paralyzed? If I was truly lucky, I wouldn't have broken my neck in the first place.

I remember once, after we had come to American and had settled in, my mother said to my father, "Could you imagine how life would have been different if we had gone to the United States before the war started? How much heartache and suffering we would have avoided."

I thought about this and said to my Mother, "I have absolutely no regrets, Mom. It happened the way it was supposed to happen."

What I meant was that because of the war, I learned how courageous my mother was. I experienced what it's like to be hungry and to be without warm clothing in the cold. These were things that were necessary to know.

My family drew close together because we all came so close to dying on that mountain top. Today, we all love each other so very much and that love flows from the well of our hardships back then.

I remember what it was like to have nothing but scraps to eat...sometimes not even that. I remember what it was like to watch my mother vanish down the mountain side and not know if I'd see her again. And I remember the joy of her return, her striding up the trails, moving as fast as she could manage to bring food back for her children. I remember her smile. It was a smile you could see for miles.

That's what life is all about. Courage and family. Honesty and commitment.

Let me leave you with one last story. Because of the many times that I had headlined at Madison Square Garden, I was invited to go visit the New York World's Fair as a special guest of the City. While I was there, the Fair's Officials wanted to have me leave the imprints of my hands in cement...for posterity. So I agreed and stuck my hands into the wet cement, pulling up

205

Relaxing at home with my grandchild.

the sleeves of my suit coat so it wouldn't get dirty.

As I wiped my hands on a towel, one of the photographers from a newspaper came up with a bright idea. He suggested that I lift up two barrels of beer that were sitting behind us and hold them in the air while everybody took a picture.

I didn't realize just how heavy these barrels were...especially with beer inside them. With the help of a few men, first one barrel was hoisted onto my left shoulder, then the other was grunted up onto my right shoulder. Because of the barrel's size and shape, I couldn't simply rest them on my shoulders. I had to wrap my arms around each one and just muscle them up. As I would adjust my position, the beer would slosh back and forth, nearly knocking me over with each swoosh.

The photographers and TV crews went wild. They loved the image...this big guy in a suit and tie, holding two giant beer barrels on his shoulders. They took picture after picture and rolled film for what seemed like an hour.

I must have been on more magazine covers than Elvis!

Everybody thought that since I was so strong, I could hold the barrels up forever. Smile, they told me. Well, I ended up in so much pain, I thought my arms were going to fall off...but I wasn't going to complain. I was determined to endure it.

Finally, everybody had enough pictures and some guys helped me get the barrels of beer back down. People came up and wanted to shake my hand and I remember I could barely lift my arm to do it.

When I got back to the hotel, I gingerly slipped off my jacket and saw that the weight of the barrels had cut into my shoulders. Blood had soaked through and stained my shirt. As I unbuttoned my shirt to attend to my wounds, I thought how great a day it had been over at the World's Fair. Everywhere I had gone, a crowd had followed. The fans had made me feel like a real celebrity.

Well, that's my story. I *did* get to live the American Dream and found out that, just as I imagined as a kid, the streets in America really *are* paved in gold.

Bruno Sammartino, today.

208

The following pages contain some additional photographs that I was unable to fit within the main text of this book but wished to share with you.

—Bruno

A favorite portrait of Carol and I attending a banquet.

211

After a bout, back in my dressing room with visitor Miguel Perez.

1965 with Monsignor Fusco, Father Rivi and John Ricchuto.

Receiving an award from Pennsylvania State Athletic Commissioner Paul G. Sullivan.

213

Talking with baseball legend Roy Campinella.

Yet another award. This time it's presented by Commissioner & Promoter Pete "Figo" Carvella as Blackie Gennaro looks on.

214

In the seventies I thought I'd try dropping a few pounds and growing a moustache

John Ricchuito, me and Father Rivi.

In Monsignor Fusco's study from left to right are Stan Marsico, John Ricchuito, me, Msr. Fusco, Henry Bellini and Fr. Rivi.

216

Enjoying some rare time at home with my son David.

217

Celebrating a birthday with my twins Daryl and Danny and my wife Carol. David was off wrestling somewhere.

218

I made several successful trips to Japan.

David poses with his two brothers.

Carol and I enjoy a night on the town.

Passing time on a train trip in Japan on the way to one of my matches.

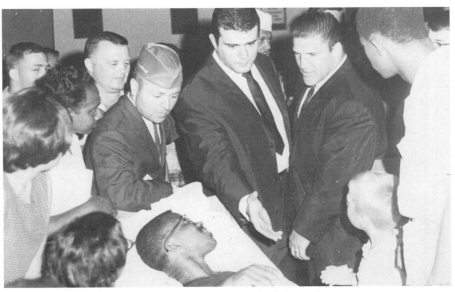

A photo from one of the many hospitals that I visited throughout my career.

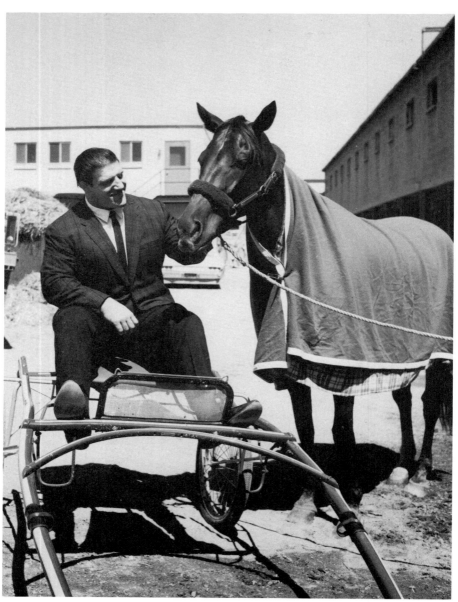

Posing with an Australian horse right before I left for one of my Australian tours.

Sports legends get together at Balleys Casino. From left to right are Phil Esposito, Johnny Unitas, me, Walt Fraser, VP of Balleys Richard Knight, Berl Rotfeld, Bobby Riggs, Brooks Robinson and Willie Mays.

With opera legend Franco Corelli.

223

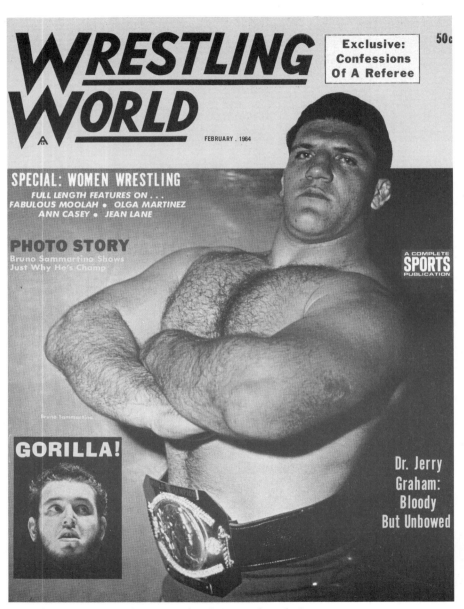

One of the many magazine covers that I appeared on during my career.

W.W.W.F. CHAMPIONSHIP WRESTLING

SANCTIONED BY THE WORLD WIDE WRESTLING FEDERATION
HISASHI SHINMA, PRESIDENT
UNDER SUPERVISION OF THE NEW YORK STATE ATHLETIC COMMISSION

OFFICIAL PROGRAM MAGAZINE #18   PRICE: $1.00

BRUNO SAMMARTINO

THE WORLD WIDE
WRESTLING FEDERATION

W.W.W.F.
HISASHI SHINMA
PRESIDENT

THE LIVING LEGEND

THE BOX OFFICE AT
MADISON SQUARE
GARDEN IS OPEN
DAILY FROM 10 TO 8

The cover of one of the many wrestling programs.

225

Practicing my backfloat in mid air! A match in 1968 with Waldo Von Erick.

Arm wrestling with singer/composer Mel Torme.

Come and get it...

Carol and I pose with Danny and Daryl. This photo was taken not too long after I had broken my neck.

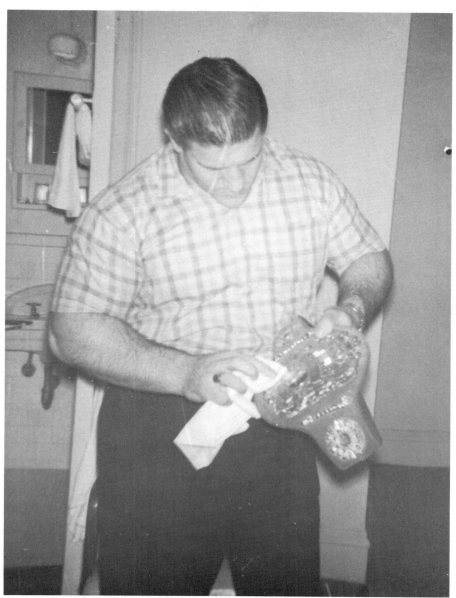

Polishing the belt I was so proud to have.

One of my matches against Don Leo Jonathan.

1973 vs. Stan Stasiak.

December 10, 1973 after regaining the belt with Vince McMahon, Sr. and Willy Gilzenberg.

In 1974, I wrestled a "masked" Killer Kowalski.

Primo Carnerra poses in our home with my Dad and me in June of 1961.

Here I am ready for action.

Here I am posing with then champion Pedro Morales.

In 1968 I crushed Ernie Ladd.

Interesting reading then...

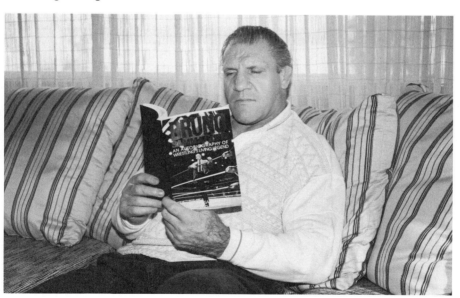

...and now.

At home at my desk still answering fan mail.

236

Bruno, Partner Win 'Snow' Job

In a revised main event, Bruno Sammartino and Dom DeNucci scored a two-fall victory over Baron Scicluna and Jim Grabmayer in 18 minutes and 12 seconds last night in a tag team wrestling match at the Civic Arena.

The announced crowd of 4,000 booed when it was announced that Stanley Stansiak was snowed in at Buffalo and wouldn't be able to face Sammartino in the scheduled main event.

In the other two matches: John DeFazio defeated Pete Yorkstrom in 10:55. Steve Bolas defeated The Executioner in 15:02.

Bruno, Ladd Wind Up Losers

There was no winner in the headliner match of the wrestling card at the Civic Arena last night.

Both Bruno Sammartino and Ernie Ladd were disqualified for fighting. Angelo Mosca and Dom DeNucci also got into the brawl and they also were tossed for a loss by the State Athletic Commission.

A crowd of 8,672 was on hand. Other results:

Dr. Bill Miller won over Waldo Von Erich, 8:24; Johnny Valentine Jr. and Chris Colt won over Luis Martinez and Johnny Furr, 16 minutes; Geeto Mongol, Al Donner and Johnny DeFazio defeated Animal) Steele, Luke

Bruno Wins Over Kowalski

Bruno Sammartino won over Killer Kowalski in the main event of the wrestling card before 4,120 fans at the Civic Arena last night. The time was 21:54.

Prof. Tanaka was disqualified in his match with Tony Parisi. The end came at 12:48 with the referee calling a halt.

Other results:

Dr. Bill Miller and Johnny DeFazio won over Tony Altomare and the Executioner, 13:26; George (The Animal) Steel won over Dom DeNucci, 14:20; Baron Scicluna won over Frank Holtz, 10:24; Ron Matteucci pinned Frank Durso 8:05.

Crusher 'Kicks' Bruno at Arena

Foul tactics, which somehow didn't disquality him, enabled Stan (Crusher) Stasiak to defeat Bruno Sammartino in the main wrestling exhibition before more than 6,000 fans at the Civic Arena last night.

Crusher kicked Bruno in the groin and he was counted out at 17 minutes 12 seconds.

Ron Matteucci decisioned John Vansky in 8:12; Walt Jowalski won over DeNucci when ths latter's bleeding referee to call a halt; Irish and Jim Grabmire bat-John DeFazio

Some clippings that appeared in the papers.

237

Bruno, Giant Win Matches

Bruno Sammartino pinned Baron Von Rashke in 14:11 and 7-4 giant Jean Andre Ferre stopped Killer Kowalski in 17:21 in feature wrestling bouts last night at the Civic Arena.

Dom DeNucci, Tony Parisi and Johnny DeFazio won over Baron Scicluna, Big Jim Grabmire and Cowboy Parker, 18:29; Luis Martinez and the Executioner drew, 15:00; Larry Zbyszko won over Frank Valois, 5:12; Frank Holtz won over Mike Loren, 10:16.

Bruno Team Wins Match

Bruno Sammartino and Dick the Bruiser defeated Baron Von Raschke and Ricky Cortez in 13:04 of the pro wrestling co-feature last night at the Civic Arena.

Pedro Morales pinned Erik the Red at 11:03 in the other main event.

Don DeNucci and Tony Parisi won over Jimmy Valiant and John L. Sullivan, 10:42; Luis Martinez pinned Bruce Swaze, 9:24; Johnny DeFazio and the Executioner, no decision, a double knockout; Frank Holtz won over Al Hays, 5:04, and Frank Durso beat Dino Nero, 7:12.

Wrestlers Cut, Match Halted

Bruno Sammartino's match with Joe LeDuc last night at the Civic Arena was halted after 14:15 because both wrestlers were bleeding from cuts over the eyes.

Ivan Koloff won over Gorilla Monsoon, 8:12; Baron Scicluna pinned Mike Palduce, 9:14; Dr. Bill Miller pinned Frank Turko, 8:12; ...

Sammartino breaks neck during bout

PITTSBURGH (AP) — World Champion heavyweight wrestler Bruno Sammartino is recuperating from a broken neck suffered during a bout Monday in New York, a local physician said Thursday.

Dr. Louis Civitrese, a longtime friend of the wrestler, said the 6-foot, 255-pound Sammartino suffered a fracture of the sixth cervical vertebra during a match with Stan Houston, a 6-foot-7, 327-pounder. The match was stopped by the referee.

Sammartino, 37, was initially treated at New York's St. Clair Hospital, but returned to Divine Providence Hospital here for treatment, said Dr. Civitrese, head of surgery at Divine Providence.

Civitrese said the wrestler is in traction and will be out of action for at least five weeks and perhaps longer.

"This can be a permanent disability, but not necessarily and I doubt it in this case," the doctor said. "There has been no damage to the spinal cord."

He said Sammartino was ambulatory when he entered the hospital here and has no loss of feeling or movement in his limbs. Sammartino lives in the Pittsburgh's North Hills area.

238